LONG LIFE TO YOUR CHILDREN!

LONG LIFE TO YOUR CHILDREN!

A Portrait of High Albania

Photographs by Stan Sherer
Text by Marjorie Senechal

The University of Massachusetts Press
AMHERST

Copyright © 1997 by Stan Sherer and Marjorie Senechal

All rights reserved

Printed in Hong Kong

LC 96-37827

ISBN 1-55849-096-5 (cloth); 097-3 (pbk.)

Book designed by Stan Sherer

Set in Adobe Garamond

Printed and bound by Everbest Printing Co. Ltd., Hong Kong

Library of Congress Cataloging-in-Publication Data

Sherer, Stan, 1947–

   Long life to your children! : a portrait of High Albania /

photographs by Stan Sherer; text by Marjorie Senechal.

      p. cm.

  Includes bibliographical references.

   ISBN 1-55849-096-5 (cloth : alk. paper). — ISBN 1-55849-097-3 (pbk. : alk. paper)

   1. Albania — Description and travel. 2. Albania — Pictorial works.

3. Sherer, Stan, 1947– — Journeys — Albania.

I. Senechal, Marjorie. II. Title.

DR918.S54 1997

914.96504' 4—dc21

96-37827
CIP

British Library Cataloguing in Publication Data are available.

Frontispiece: Theth at dusk.

For Elpinike Frasher

Contents

LONG LIFE TO YOUR CHILDREN!

Waiting for a truck,
Theth center.

Introduction

THE JAGGED PEAKS OF THE ACCURSED MOUNTAINS glittered in the bright morning sunlight. We sat on large rocks in the shade of a tree in what once was the center of Theth, in the almost inaccessible Dukagjin region of northern Albania. Together with about half a dozen Albanians from Theth and nearby villages, we were listening for a truck that would take us to the city of Shkoder (listening, rather than looking: you can hear those old Czech or Chinese vehicles that ply these mountains long before you can see them). The one hundred kilometer trip, when it finally began, would take four or five hours along a twisting, unpaved, single-lane road through forests and over mountain passes, with frequent stops to pick up logs. For a brief time – in the communist era – there had been bus service to and from this region, but in 1994 buses ran where and when and if their driver-owners chose to go, and they didn't choose to go to the northern mountains. That left a ride in the back of a truck as the only form of public transportation in this part of the country; it wasn't too bad when the weather was good. There was no longer mail or telephone service in the mountains, but a few mountain families had managed to buy satellite dishes, and television brought the world into their living rooms. Although geographically isolated, mountain communities were not isolated from the rapid changes taking place in Albania.

The high school student waiting with us was eager to practice her English: she spoke very well although she had been studying for only a year. "And what," she asked politely, "do Americans think of our president, Sali Berisha?" The question conveyed her pride in Albania's becoming, at last, a nation among others, a nation like others. How could I explain to her that few Americans can tell Albania from Albany or Alabama, and fewer still would be able to find her country on the map? I tried to be tactful: "I'm sorry, but I don't think that most Americans know who Albania's president is," and quickly changed the subject by asking her the Albanian names for the plants around us. Eventually a rattling, grumbling, elderly truck pulled up near the tree and all conversation gave way to the continuous task of finding stable and not hopelessly uncomfortable positions on the pile of logs that grew higher with each stop. When we finally arrived in Shkoder, in the late afternoon, the girl and her family vanished into the busy streets.

But we were asked this question, and others like it, again and again. Many of the Albanians we met during our three months in the north in the summer of 1994 were hurt and puzzled by what they perceived as the world's lack of interest in, or even awareness of, their efforts to become a modern, democratic, European nation. The problem is not new. "Oh, I know all about the Albanians, they are those funny people with pink eyes and white hair!" a woman told the intrepid British chronicler of Balkan life, Edith Durham, over ninety years ago. It would not be difficult to assemble a good-sized collection of equally absurd remarks today. Durham, who traveled on foot and by horseback throughout the north, was known as the "Queen of the Mountains" and is still fondly remembered there. The feeling was mutual: she devoted her life to making her countrymen aware of Albania and its concerns (her classic *High Albania* remains essential reading). But Albania has not had many clear-eyed chroniclers since Durham.

1

Despite its spectacular and varied beauty, its rich natural resources, and its extraordinary tradition of hospitality, Albania has always been the most isolated country in Europe, and from World War II until very recently, one of the most isolated countries on earth. Although it has been inhabited since remote antiquity – the land was part of ancient Illyria – it has never been an easy place to visit. In earlier times, travelers were hindered by nonexistent mountain roads and generally poor conditions, conditions that improved little in the five hundred years of Turkish rule. Roads were built between the two world wars and the country was electrified after World War II, but its borders were sealed (to most Westerners) after 1945. Since 1991, Albania has welcomed foreign visitors but, as the poorest country in Europe, it has attracted relatively few of them.

Yet there are many reasons why the outside world should be interested in Albania and concerned for its future. Albania is a Balkan country and thus a crossroads of East and West, North and South; it is as rich in history as it is in resources. When Albania finally achieved independence, after the collapse of the Ottoman Empire, nearly half its population found itself outside its newly drawn borders, in what is now called "the former Yugoslavia." But Albanians are not Slavs, and the Albanian language is not Slavic – it is a twigless branch on the Indo-European linguistic tree. Today large numbers of ethnic Albanians are struggling with minority status in Serbia and Macedonia, a volatile situation that the U. S. media largely ignores. Internally, Albania is a cross-section of several time periods coexisting uneasily in the present unstable conditions. It is a social tinderbox: economic shock therapy is rapidly creating new classes and widening gulfs between them. Approximately thirty percent of the workforce is unemployed; in order to feed their families, large numbers of Albanian citizens – including many professionals – work at menial jobs in Greece (legally or illegally) and in Italy. Albania's relations with all its Balkan neighbors are intermittently tense. Albania is multi-religious but not multi-ethnic. Although many Albanians insist that there is no religious tension because "the true religion of Albania is Albanianism," the actual situation is somewhat more complex.

Much has been written about the historic "transition" from communism now underway in Eastern Europe, but Albania's transition is ignored in most of these accounts. This is probably because Albania's brand of communism was different from the others, and its society is more difficult for a Westerner to understand. While it has encountered most of the problems that other postcommunist societies are confronting – industrial pollution being the significant exception – there are several factors that make Albania's experience unique.

First, although Albania became a communist state shortly after the end of the Second World War, it was not part of the "East bloc" after its break with the Soviet Union in 1961. From the mid-sixties to the mid-seventies, Albania was closely allied with China. In the spirit of socialist brotherhood, Albanian leaders tried to convince the public to drink tea, but this effort had no lasting effect: strong Turkish coffee accompanied by fiery home-brewed *raki* continued (and continues) to be the national drink. More seriously and disastrously, Albania underwent a harrowing "cultural revolution." Political and personal repression were greater in Albania than in any other European communist country.

Second, under communism Albania's natural geographical isolation was reinforced by political decree: sources of information from the outside world were strictly controlled, only a very few Albanians were permitted to travel abroad, and almost no one was allowed to visit from the West. As one Albanian friend put it, after the alliance with the Chinese Albania was surrounded by two iron curtains. The result is a nation of geopolitical and, to some extent, economic Rip Van Winkles, while for most outsiders Albania hardly exists.

Woman hoeing,
Fushe Kruje.

3

Playing soccer, Tirane

The third special factor is that the Albanians themselves set their country back many years when the communist regime ended in 1991. Citizens went on a destructive rampage, destroying schools, clinics, libraries, and other public buildings, and cutting down the trees along boulevards and in parks. Livestock was carried off from the collective farms, greenhouses were smashed, shops were looted. Who was behind this, and why? None of the many and varied explanations we have heard seems convincing to us.

And finally, although Albania has been influenced by its neighbors and by its many occupiers over the centuries, Albanian culture – like the Albanian language – has preserved a unique identity. Among the sturdy threads in its cultural tapestry are the codes of customary law that have governed social interaction since ancient times. These codes vary from region to region both in detail and in strictness; the most rigid of them is the code of the north, the *kanun* of Lek Dukagjini, which prescribes the details of inter- and intra-family relations, property, commerce, and much more, including the infamous blood feuds. The *kanun* is one of the most fascinating (but perhaps the least known) of the ancient legal systems that have come down to us. While many if not most Albanians claim that it is a long-abandoned relic of the past, we could see many ways, both positive and negative, in which it still influences life in the entire area we visited.

We became interested in Albania about ten years ago, through the novels of the Albanian writer Ismail Kadare. Kadare, who now divides his time between Paris and the Albanian capital, Tirane, is a somewhat controversial figure in his home country, but for an outsider his novels, which retell Albanian legends, reconstruct major historical events, and describe more recent affairs, are an excellent introduction to a fascinating country. I came across *Chronicle in Stone* by chance while browsing in a bookstore near our home. I started reading it that evening, and read straight through to the end. Kadare's description of his childhood in wartime Gjirokaster transported me to a strange stone city where deep cisterns held dark secrets, where the faces of brides were powdered and decorated with exotic images, where young people struggled to free themselves – and their country – from ancient customs, superstitions, and a stifling social order. As Kadare portrayed it, Albanian culture was a rare but sturdy plant that had managed to survive centuries of isolation, grafting, and trampling, to blossom in the modern world. My husband became fascinated too, and learning more about Albania became a preoccupation.

Ten years ago it was impossible for Westerners to visit Albania except perhaps on a closely guided tour, and that is not the way we like to travel. But our interest in Albania continued to grow, so we started studying the language through tapes in hopes of eventually visiting on our own. In 1992, after independent visiting had become possible, we flew from Zurich to Tirane for a two-week trip. We had arranged to spend the first few days with a family in Tirane, friends of friends in New York. Beyond that, we had no detailed plans; it was clear we would need to be flexible. Getting around was not easy: the trains were in very poor condition, so were many of the buses, and it was a test of endurance and athletic skill to get a seat. But we were lucky: we found a driver to take us, for a reasonable price, to the city of Shkoder, in the north, and young friends in Tirane climbed through a bus window to claim seats for us for a trip to Gjirokaster, in the south. A network of generous friends arranged for us to stay with Albanian families in both cities, instead of in hotels.

Through our hosts, and through our own wanderings about these cities, we were able to meet and talk with a wide variety of people. Conversation is an Albanian art form: everywhere we went people were eager to discuss everything from comparative family life to their experiences under the dictatorship to contemporary world affairs. Albania is not a third-world country, we were assured: instead, it is the fourth world. Our friend was probably joking, but "fourth world" is

Domestic courtyard,
Gjirokaster.

a succinct label for a society. in which once-functioning but now collapsed industry, agriculture, and infrastructure contrast sharply with a literate and well-educated population and spectacular natural beauty.

The two weeks flew by. We soon found that we no longer noticed the poverty that had struck us so forcibly at first: the potholes, the crumbling facades, the broken windows. We were almost able to ignore the oppressive heat (heightened by what must be a cultural prohibition against cross ventilation). Instead, we delighted in our new friends and the new world we were discovering. Even before we left, we began making plans for a much longer stay, during which we would try to use our professional talents to do something to contribute to Albania.

But how could we help? Albanians need no lessons from us in our professions, photography and mathematics. We finally decided that the most useful thing we could do, at this time, would be to try to make a dent in the general indifference: we would introduce Albania and Albanians to the world through a book of photographs and interviews. A Fulbright research fellowship (for Stan) made it possible for us to return for the summer of 1994. All too aware that three months is not long enough to begin to understand another culture, much less to portray it, we decided to spend the entire time in just one part of the country, in the hope of being able to peer beneath its surface.

We chose the region known as High Albania, in part because we had found it so intriguing on our earlier visit. High Albania includes the city of Shkoder (also known as Scutari), its outlying villages, and the Dinaric Alps. The contrasts between life in the city, in the villages around Shkoder, and in the villages in the mountains are very striking. Shkoder, an ancient city with a strong Italian – and Roman Catholic – influence, is widely regarded as the "cradle of northern Albanian culture:" the birthplace of scholars, diplomats, writers, and artists. The villages are known for colorful embroidered and handwoven clothing; in them, and also in the streets of Shkoder, one sees a fascinating mix of traditional and contemporary dress. The mountain villages, famous for their inhabitants' strict adherence to the *kanun* of Lek Dukagjini, were almost inaccessible until roads were built after World War II; none of the many invaders, not even the Turks, could impress their customs or governance on these mountain communities. We wanted to understand and explain how the various components of this society viewed their present lives and the future at this crucial time in its history.

As on our first visit, friends introduced us to friends who introduced us to friends. Again, we were privileged to live with families everywhere we went, both in Shkoder and in the mountain regions we visited, Malesi e Madhe and Dukagjin. (On this trip, we traveled mostly by bicycle and by truck.) We spoke with people of all ages and in many walks of life – shopkeepers, government officials, peasants, workers, entrepreneurs, the unemployed, pensioners, young people, children, educators, scientists, artists and writers, doctors, clergy, smugglers. Everyone received us graciously and talked with us about their daily lives – family, work, education, religion, health care, the arts – and especially about the ways in which their lives are changing and the problems they are facing as a result. They generously agreed to be photographed, and most of them allowed our conversations to be recorded.

After our return to the United States, as we studied the contact sheets of hundreds of photographic images and pages and pages of transcripts of conversations, we realized that together our acquaintances had sketched a broad portrait of northern Albania in the twentieth century. This suggested that the book should be arranged chronologically, a pattern we have followed for the most part. Chapter One is background material, Chapter Two is concerned largely with the past, Chapter Three with the present, and Chapter Four with the future. An appendix includes maps, a glossary of Albanian words, and a bibliography.

Village women entering shop, Shkoder.

Our young friend in Theth will probably be disappointed that the readers of this book will not learn anything about Albania's president. Nor will you learn much about any Albanian politician, past or present. This book is not about politics in the immediate sense. But ultimately the politics of any country is an expression of its history, its culture, and its economy. The concerns of Albanians today will shape their politics of tomorrow.

But Albania is not only a country of problems, it is a country of toasts. We have used some of them as the titles of chapters of this book. The haunting toast "Long Life to Your Children!" is especially poignant in this uncertain time, but it is also a declaration of hope.

This book is our toast, for long life and success, to our Albanian friends and their children.

CHAPTER ONE

HIGH ALBANIA

On Lake Vau i Dejes.

Illyria, Albania, Shqiperia

Hills of the Gajtan caves.

THE VILLAGE OF GAJTAN is an easy bicycle ride from Shkoder. Like many northern Albanian villages, it has no recognizable village center: you know you are there only because the map says you must be, or because a villager tells you so. In the summertime, the widely-scattered stone houses are shaded by grape vines and fruit trees, but the hilly, barren, countryside broils under the ferocious sun. We first visited Gajtan with our friend Dr. Anton Fistani, the founder and director of the Laboratory of Human Paleontology at the University of Shkoder. Anton has made important discoveries in the caves that dot the hills here, including animal bones half a million years old and stone tools left there about seven hundred thousand years ago by *Homo Erectus*. He also found a curious stone, incised with deep, carefully drawn lines; evidently it was used as a tally-stick, for counting. Carbon-14 dating at the University of Texas has shown it to be thirty two thousand five hundred seventy years old. Civilization in what is now Albania has a very long history; if its ancient sites were properly cared for, Albania would be a veritable archeological theme park.

The identity of the most ancient cultures is still debated, but any history of Albania must include the Illyrians, a collection of loosely-related tribes that spread throughout the Balkans in prehistoric times. Illyrians may or may not have been Albania's original inhabitants; in any case, the name Albania comes from that of an Illyrian tribe, the Albani. (But in the Albanian language, the name of the country is *Shqiperia*, the name of the language is *shqip*, and the Albanians are *shqiptare*.)

Illyrian ruins abound throughout Albania. Later in the summer we climbed a hill near the Gajtan caves with Fatbardha Mataj, an engineer at the nearby Vau i Dejes hydropower station, and her brother-in-law, looking for the site of a fortress thought to have been built by the Illyrian Labeates tribe about 1000 BCE (around the time that they founded the city of Shkoder). The fort is not visible from the village and there are no signs pointing to it, but people living nearby indicated the general direction. As we ascended the barely discernible path to the summit, we saw more and more stones, large and small, scattered everywhere. Eventually the scattering began to seem less random, and finally we came across some well-built steps and a long, wide wall that suggested a once-magnificent edifice. Through a fine doorway in the wall, we could see rich farmland to the east and, far beyond that, the artificial lake Vau i Dejes, constructed in the early 1970's by the

Illyrian citadel, Gajtan.

Chinese in conjunction with the station. Building the fortress must have been a comparable feat of Illyrian technology. Where did they get these enormous stones, and how did they haul them all the way up here? I tried to imagine adult Illyrians working and talking, Illyrian children playing; I wished I could ask them about their lives. But there was only silence. No one lives there now, though occasionally goats wander by.

Archaeologists and historians have shown that Illyrian culture varied according to the diverse geography of the Balkans. Some Illyrians were semi-nomads, living with their animals in high mountain pastures in the summer, bringing them back down to the valleys in the winter. This pattern of seasonal migration is still followed today in the mountains of High Albania; we visited several families in their summer sheds.

Other Illyrians were settled farmers who cultivated a variety of fruits, cereals, and vegetables, produced clothing, and worked mines. The Illyrians left no written record of their language, but some scholars believe that it evolved into modern Albanian. Others believe it did not.

Thus we step into the minefield of Albanian history. "The history of Albania, a complicated tale of extreme interest, remains to be written – strange that it should be so," wrote Edith Durham in 1909. Much has been written since then, but Durham's remarks may still be true. Every detail of Albania's history is controversial. Some excellent books are beginning to appear now, but there are still gaps and contradictions in the story. The archives of the Ottoman Empire are only now becoming accessible. A great deal of historical research was done by Albanians in the communist era, but the objectivity of some of this work is open to question.

Nevertheless, some readers may appreciate a little background material on the history of Albania, especially northern Albania, the setting of this book. This chapter summarizes our understanding of the developments and events to which the people speaking in these pages allude. It is sketchy and incomplete, but we hope that it is not misleading, and that it will be a useful supplement to the next three chapters.

Some conventions. We use the name "Albania" for the land that is now modern Albania, although this is an historical anachronism. We also use the modern Albanian names for cities, even though in some cases their names were different in the past. For example what is now the city of Shkoder was the Scodra of the Illyrians and the Romans, and then for many centuries was widely known as Scutari. Today's Durres was the Roman Dyrrachium, later Durazzo. We use BCE and CE ("before the common era" and "common era") in place of BC and AD ("Before Christ" and "Anno Domini," the Year of the Lord). Albanian words are italicized (see the glossary). Instead of indicating references by numbered footnotes, we give the initials of the author next to the quotation and the full citation in the bibliography.

Tone Smajlaj in her
summer shed, Koprisht.

13

Albania before the Ottoman conquest. One continuous theme in Albanian history has been the interplay between the unity of the people (reinforced by language, culture and history) on the one hand and on the other a marked distinction between the north and the south. This theme has its roots in antiquity. By 700 BCE there were Greek settlements as well as Illyrian ones along the southern coast; this intermingling of cultures influenced the development of society in the southern region, while northern Albania, the region we are interested in here, remained wholly Illyrian. The largest city in the north, Shkoder, was an Illyrian center for almost 1000 years. Founded by the Labaeates, it had become the capital of another Illyrian tribe, the Ardiaeans, by about 400 BCE. The Ardiaeans were notorious for piracy and for their raids on western Greece; at least that is how the Romans viewed them. In the third century BCE, "They had an extremely able and heroic queen, Teuta, who was not the sort of monarch that can be raised from a tribe in skins," writes Rebecca West in *Black Lamb and Grey Falcon*, "and while she and her subjects are accused of piracy, examination proves this a reference to efforts, which history would regard as creditable if they had been undertaken by the Romans, to conquer the Adriatic archipelago."(RW)

But history is written by the victors. In 229 BCE, after a major battle in which Teuta's forces were defeated, a treaty was concluded in Rome. "The terms of the settlement were conveyed to the Leagues in Greece," writes John Wilkes in *The Illyrians*, "where they were well received since 'the Illyrians were not the enemies of this or that people, but the common enemies of all alike' (Polybius 2.12). So ended the first Roman action against Illyrians." Eighty years later, in 169 BCE, Gentius, the last king of the Illyrians, surrendered at Shkoder. Albania was folded into the Roman Empire.

The Romans brought the material blessings of their civilization to Albania, including amphitheaters and roads. The most important of these roads was the Via Egnatia, which linked the port cities of Durres and Appolonia with the inland city of Elbasan, and then continued on to Thessalonika and Byzantium. Thus a major trade route was cut through Albania, stimulating the development of the interior. Like the Ottomans over 1500 years later, the Romans divided the country to keep it under control. The Ardiaean kingdom was divided into three parts: north, central, and south. The northern part included Shkoder and the Albanian Alps, although the inaccessible Alps were never completely conquered by the Romans. When the Roman Empire was divided in 395, what is now Albania became part of the Eastern Empire, Byzantium.

The next thousand years saw almost continuous warfare, beginning with invasions by Visigoths, Huns, and Ostrogoths in the fifth century. The Slav invasions began in the sixth century, and Albania was dominated by the Slavs from the seventh century to the ninth; indeed, the Slavs dominated the northern highlands until the time of the Turks. (At this point another persistent theme of Albanian history enters the picture: resistance to its Slav neighbors.) After Byzantine authority was reasserted, Bulgarian invasions began; Durres was captured by Bulgaria by the end of the tenth century. One hundred years later Albania was devastated by the first Crusade. As Byzantine authority weakened, various forms of the name "Albania" began to be used for the region. Byzantine rule finally ended in the 1340's, around the time that the Serbian Empire was established. By 1347 Albania was under Serbian control.

The Albanian hero Skanderbeg. In 1389 the Serbian King Lazar was defeated and killed by the forces of Sultan Murad I (who also died during the battle). Lazar's defeat, on the Plain of Kosova, is considered by moderns Serbs to be the one of the most important events in their history; this is one of the reasons why Kosove, now largely populated by Albanians, is a highly contentious area today. In fact, the army that lost that battle in 1389 was a united army of many Balkan peoples, including Albanians. Afterwards there was disarray everywhere. The Venetians occupied the Alba-

In the courtyard of Skanderbeg's castle, Kruje.

15

nian coastal towns in 1396 (in Shkoder they built Rozafa Castle, on the site of earlier fortifications). Most of the rest of Albania became a vassal of the Ottoman Empire, though it was not immediately incorporated into it.

Ottoman invasions of Albania had begun in 1385, but Albania did not fall until 1468. The story is a complex one involving Venetian and Byzantine, as well as Turkish, interests, and the strong desire of Albania's feudal lords to maintain such independence as they had. It is likely that Albania would have surrendered years earlier had it not been for the heroism and leadership of its most famous native son, Gjergj Kastrioti, also known as Skanderbeg. Gjergj was born in 1405; his father Gjon was a feudal lord who, in 1423, placed himself and his lands at Kruje under the protection of Sultan Murad II. (Gjon seems to have been a very flexible man, changing his religion – not once but several times – as easily as Americans change jobs and houses.)

As Fan Noli explains in his biography, *George Castrioti Skanderbeg (1405–1468)*, there are conflicting accounts of Gjergj's early life. In those days, a certain percentage of the young Christian boys in the Sultan's realms were taken, each year, from their homes to the court, where they were raised as Muslims and educated to be members of the elite Janissary corps. Some of these boys rose to high positions in the Ottoman Empire. So did Gjergj, although it is not clear whether he was a young boy or a young man when he went to the Sultan, or whether he was taken in the annual roundup or sent there by his father. In any case, the name Skanderbeg comes from the name he was given at court, Iskender (Alexander); beg was an honorary title. Skanderbeg did not remain loyal to the Sultan very long. Upon Gjon's death, the Sultan claimed the Kastrioti lands for his own. Gjergj, who had until then fought battles on the Ottoman side, returned to Albania to reclaim his father's property. He succeeded in this, but that is not wherein his greatness lies. Skanderbeg organized the feudal lords in opposition to the Ottomans and, under his leadership, they fended off repeated incursions for twenty five years, until his death in 1468. This period marks the beginning of Albanian national consciousness, and Skanderbeg is revered today for creating the Albanian nation. After Skanderbeg's death, the Albanian resistance collapsed; Shkoder was the last Albanian city to fall, in 1479. The Kastrioti family (and other leading families) fled to Italy.

Skanderbeg was a hero in his own lifetime, celebrated as the last Balkan crusader. Yet he seems to have been a modest man. "The city of Rome accorded him a triumphal entry. Skanderbeg, however, did not enter the city like a medieval commander, in elegant armor. The chronicles note that he was 'clad like a poor man,' even though at that juncture he was the best known of all Europe's commanders."(JM) The Skanderbeg legend has been told and retold in many forms and many languages; in English, Henry Wadsworth Longfellow recounted it (up to his seizure of his father's lands) in *Tales of a Wayside Inn*. Today Skanderbeg's statue dominates the center of Tirane and his castle at Kruje is a popular tourist site.

Twenty four years after Skanderbeg's death, Columbus landed in America. An Albanian friend, innocent of political correctness, explained the subsequent history of Albania thus: "Europe brought civilization to America just as five centuries of darkness descended upon us."

Social organization. In the Ottoman Empire, all land belonged to the Sultan. Most of Albania was placed in a single administrative unit known as a *sandjak*. The *sandjak* was divided into *vilayets*, whose governors could issue *timars*, or fiefs, for military or civil service. Although in principle the fiefs could neither be sold nor inherited, they "were gradually transformed into *ciftliks* (estates). At the same time the system of farming out the state lands in the lowlands, the coastal plains, and the interior basins, created in Albania a class of big landowners."(SS1) But, like the Romans, the Turks were never able to govern the northern mountains. Throughout the five hundred years of "the

Ottoman yoke," the ancient social organization of the highlands continued apparently unchanged from ancient times. The fundamental unit of society was the *fis*, which can be translated as "kin:" a *fis* consisted of one or more extended families. At the next level was the *bajrak* (a Turkish word that means banner, or standard), composed of one or more *fises*; the head of the *bajrak* was the *bajraktar*. An aggregation of *bajraks* was a tribe. One's place in this extended family network determined one's identity. Elsewhere in Albania, the social organization was much looser, but identification of the individual with the family was also very strong; indeed, it is still strong today.

The Ottomans gave special privileges to those who would convert to Islam, and many Albanians did, especially in the southern and central regions. "The majority of Albanians, being Moslems, enjoyed a privileged position in the empire, from which their Orthodox and Catholic countrymen were barred. This contrast in status between Christians and Moslems constituted a serious hindrance to unification" (SS1). It still plays a role in Albanian political life, especially in the north. So does the continuing division between north and south, which the Ottomans exacerbated by playing the *pashas* or *beys* [*bey* and *beg* are the same word] off against one another, and also the chieftains of the highlands. Meanwhile, two local dynasts emerged, the Bushatis in the north and Ali Pasha Tepelena in the south, which eventually grew to hereditary principalities.

Education was not a priority in the Ottoman Empire, but by the second half of the seventeenth century there were Turkish schools for boys and also *medreses*, Islamic religious schools. Orthodox boys attended Greek schools; Albanian-language schools were forbidden. Catholic schools (taught in Italian or Latin) were established, in the north, only in 1855, two centuries later. Girls did not attend school at all until the twentieth century; the position of women in Albania was traditionally a subordinate one (see the section on the *kanun* of Lek Dukagjini).

Religion. "Christianity reached the western side of the [Balkan] peninsula at an early date, via the sea . . . Titus, St. Paul's disciple, went to Dalmatia. St. Paul himself preached the Gospel in Illyria. The Roman coast towns, Salona, Scutari, and Durazzo, were early centres from which Christianity radiated . . . Illyria naturally formed part of the Patriarchate of Rome, and portions of Illyria have remained faithful to this day." (ED1) But what sort of religion had the Illyrians practiced before the arrival of Christianity? As John Wilkes explains, the Illyrians seem not to have had any formalized religion, with ritual practices, but they did acknowledge supernatural forces and attributed control over the vicissitudes of daily life to the power of deities. Their ornament contains a wide variety of symbols, especially the sun. (Sun cults were popular in many parts of the ancient world, including Rome itself.) The Illyrians were avid tattooers, and sun symbols were popular tattoos. Sun symbols continued to be etched into gravestones in northern Albania until this century.

Some early Balkan rituals evolved smoothly into Christian ones; for example, Edith Durham suggests that the concept of holy water may have had its symbolic source in the pagan propitiation of the god of the spring. In Yugoslavia, holy trees became sacred Christian sites, carved with the cross. Processions around these trees were held each year. Such holy "log places" still exist in Albania, at least in memory; in one recent court case (see p. 154) residents objected to the private use of one such place as a site for a cafe.

Gravestone symbols, early 20th C., from Edith Durham, "Some Tribal Origins, Laws, and Customs of the Balkans."

With the Church schism in 1054, northern Albania remained Catholic, while southern Albania – long influenced by Greek Orthodoxy – became Orthodox, and "the feudal lords . . . led an amphibious life between Catholicism and Orthodoxy."(SS1)

Islam entered Albania with the Ottomans. At first, the Ottomans did not demand the conversion of the feudal lords, as long as they paid tribute, sent their sons to the court, and supplied troops when needed. But later the Islamic religion was introduced, gradually at first and then more rapidly.

> The Bosnians and Herzegovinians – the Bosnians more especially – adopted Islam in many cases as early as the fifteenth century, whereas the Albanians, upon whom it sits far more lightly, and a very large number of whom belong to the heretical Bektashi sect, became Mohammedan mainly in the seventeenth and eighteenth centuries, and some in the nineteenth. The women of the Moslem Albanian mountain tribes are never veiled, and will come to market and bargain freely with any man, their faces more exposed than those of many Christians.(ED1)

It is said that today approximately seventy percent of Albanians are Muslim, twenty percent Orthodox, and ten percent Catholic; in the north the population is half Catholic, half Muslim.

During the communist era, the government at first tried to persuade the churches to break their foreign ties, which it saw as threats to Albanian independence. For example, a priest who survived imprisonment recalls,

> Enver Hoxha then summoned Archbishop Gasper Thaci, the metropolitan of Shkoder and primate of Albania, and Archbishop Vincenc Prendushi of Durres for a meeting. Hoxha requested the separation of the Albanian Church from Rome, a constitution of a national Church and Church adherence to the new regime. In return he offered a 'conciliatory attitude' and material help to support the ecclesiastical institutions. The two prelates courageously refused to adhere to those proposals. They paid for this refusal with their lives. Monsignor Thaci died in 1946 while he was under house arrest. Monsignor Prendushi was condemned to twenty years of hard labor. He died in prison in 1949 after being savagely tortured.(GG)

Some of the Catholic-Muslim tension in the north today derives at least in part from the conviction of some Catholic Shkodrans that the communists, many of whom came from Muslim backgrounds, had singled out the Catholic population for special persecution. In 1967, the government abolished all religion. Mosques and churches were closed; many were destroyed or put to other uses, such as stores or sport halls. Albania became the world's only officially atheist state.

There have been Jews in Albania since ancient times. Edith Durham tells of meeting people in the mountains who were sure that the land there had once belonged to the Jews. She knew of no basis for this claim, but we have learned – from a small booklet called *The Jews of Albania*, by Harvey Sarner – that there may be archeological evidence of Jewish communities in the north in ancient times. Other Jews came after their expulsion from Spain in 1492. (In the seventeenth century, the false messiah Sabbatai Zevi was exiled to Albania by a Turkish sultan; his grave is a holy site for Bektashi Muslims.) In the nineteenth century, Jews immigrated from Greece. Though few in number, the Jews of Albania were prosperous. Almost all of them survived the Nazi occupation, thanks to the courage of their Muslim and Christian neighbors. After the war, the communists confiscated the property of all wealthy people, including that of the Jews, and they became poor like everybody else. There seems to have been no antisemitism in Albania, just the opposite: the Jews and their non-Jewish neighbors were very close and intermarriage was common. After the end of communism, almost the entire Albanian Jewish community emigrated to Israel.

Language and literature. Until comparatively recently, the Albanian language was largely an oral language, not a written one. The first historical reference to Albanian writing seems to be a 1332 letter from the Dominican friar, Brochart, to Philippe de Valois, king of France, in which he noted that " . . . although the Albanians [of the north] have a language quite different from that of the Latins, they use the Latin letters in all their books." For the next five centuries, books written in the Albanian language were few and far between, and those few were ecclesiastical.

But although its written literature was slight, over the centuries Albania developed a magnificent oral literature in the epic tradition. In the northern mountains, there are still *rapsods*, or singers of tales, today (see pp. 70-71). As in every oral tradition, the Albanian songs change over time and with the individual singer, making it difficult – but not impossible – to trace their origin. Ismail Kadare's novel, *The Dossier H* (which has been translated into French but not yet into English) is, among other things, an amusing story of two American folklorists who visit Albania to try to prove that the songs of the north are directly descended from the songs of Homer. They are unable to establish their hypothesis, but they do reach the conclusion that the Albanian songs are older than their Serbian counterparts. The Americans' work comes to naught through the machinations of a furious Serb who does not want their discovery to see the light of day.

> The Albanian heroic songs are called, among the northern mountaineers, 'slant songs' or 'songs on the edge of the wing', but a more general term for them is 'songs of valor.' The greater part of the songs of ' valor' tell of events and episodes in a particular section of the Albanian world. They are like chronicles. Vendetta murder is chiefly their subject, but there may also be murder for the protection on of women . . . treason is another topic . . . or clashes between Turkish authorities and Albanian mountaineers."SS2

Heroic epic ballads were (and are) accompanied on the *lahute*, a one-stringed instrument something like a dulcimer (see pp. 70, 219), or on the two-stringed, long-necked *cifteli*. Albanian epics began to attract the interest of European scholars in the second half of the nineteenth century; since then, many collections – of varying authenticity – have been published, but only a few of the songs have been translated into English.

Turkish, Greek, and Italian were the written languages of the educated classes. When Albanian was written, at least three alphabets were used: Catholics used the Latin alphabet, Orthodox the Greek, and Muslims the Arabic. Not only were there several scripts, there were two (mutually intelligible) dialects, Gheg in the north, Tosk in the south. Thus Albanian written literature developed slowly and late; Pjeter Budi's *Christian Doctrine* (1618) was one of the first books written in Albanian. Albanian was first taught in a Jesuit secondary school, the College of St. Francis, which opened in Shkoder in 1877 (but the language of instruction was Italian). The first Albanian school for boys opened in Korçe in 1885, and the first Albanian school for girls, also in Korçe, in 1891. As Albanian national awareness grew, the standardization of the alphabet became a pressing need. After much discussion and negotiation, the Latin alphabet was formally adopted in 1909. (See the glossary in the Appendix.)

The standardization of the Albanian alphabet was not accompanied by a standardization of the Albanian language. The two main dialects continued to reflect the north/south division, and Albanian grammar had scarcely been mapped. Even today, after years of intensive and systematic study by Albanians and foreigners

Verbali i nënshkruem nga Antarët e Komisjonit për caktimin e Alfabetit të Gjuhës shqipe.

Report of the Commission on the Albanian Alphabet, 1909.

19

alike, Albanian grammar seems uncomfortably stuffed into the standard Indo-European straight-jacket of conjugations and declensions. Beginning in the 1950's, efforts were made to standardize both the spoken and written language, but this standardization was (and still is) highly controversial in the north, as many Ghegs believed that the standard language was in fact Tosk and that the choice had been made on political grounds, reflecting the Tosk background of many leading communists.

From "Turkey-in-Europe" to modern Albania. Albania's relationship with the Ottoman Empire was more complex than that of most of its neighbors, in part because the landowning *pashas* and *beys* had a vested interest in their privileges, which derived from the Ottomans. Thus although they were jealous of their rights, "independence was far from their political thinking."(ss1) Besides, the Turks offered protection against Albania's Slavic neighbors to the north. Religious and geographical differences also slowed the development of a national awareness. But in the nineteenth century, awareness grew steadily, although more slowly than in other Ottoman-occupied lands. With awareness came revolts and uprisings.

Many of the heroic figures of this period in Albanian history came from the north. Two of those recalled by people you will meet in this book are Bajram Curri (1862–1925) and Luigj Gurakuqi (1879–1925).

Bajram Curri was an Albanian from Kosove; he played a leading role in the nationalist movement and later was a prominent member of the Popular Party, led by Fan Noli (about whom see below). He briefly served as Minister of War in the 1921 government led by fellow Kosovar Hassan Pristina. Curri was a bitter enemy of Ahmed Zogu (also see below); when Zog seized power in 1922, Curri was sentenced to death, in absentia, by a military court. There are conflicting stories of Curri's death; the most dramatic of them is relayed in *The Blue Guide*:

> "Curri was eventually gunned down by Zog's police in the Dragobi cave, in truly heroic circumstances, fighting his enemies to the last, a smoking pistol in hand, and with loyal followers from his *fis* surrounding him."

Today you can visit the cave, near the town named for him.

Luigj Gurakuqi, a Catholic intellectual from Shkoder, joined the 1911 rebellion of the northern mountains against the Turks and was instrumental in the negotiations that established Albania's independence. In 1924 he served as Minister of Economy and Finance in the short-lived government of Fan Noli. He too was assassinated on orders of Zog. Gurakuqi had been the director of the Teachers' School in Elbasan, which opened in 1909; the University Luigj Gurakuqi in Shkoder is named for him. His statue stands in the center of Shkoder.

On the eve of World War I, the Ottoman Empire was collapsing and the map of Southern Europe was being redrawn. Albania's neighbors, Serbia, Montenegro, and Greece, were eager to help themselves to slices of it. Albania declared its independence on November 28, 1912, in the southern city of Vlore, and raised Skanderbeg's emblem – a black double-headed eagle against a red background – as its national flag. (Since then, November 28 has been celebrated as Flag Day by Albanians throughout the world.) Although a government had been formed under the leadership of Ismail Qemal, the world took little notice of it. The following year, the London Conference of Ambassadors agreed that Albania should be an independent state but awarded large portions of it to its hungry neighbors; they also selected an inexperienced German Prince, William of Wied, to rule Albania. Wied's government was ineffectual and he left after six months. That year, the last Turkish troops left Albanian soil, but Albania's troubles were not over. (The suffering of the northern mountain people in the subsequent battles with Montenegro are recounted in Edith Durham's harrowing, breathless memoir, *The Struggle for Scutari*.) In 1914, the Albanian flag was raised at Rozafa Castle in Shkoder, but soon after that the Austrian Archduke Francis Ferdinand was assassinated in Sarejevo, unleashing World War I, and Albania was up for grabs again.

That Albania's independence and territorial integrity were preserved owes much to the efforts of President Woodrow Wilson, who is still revered in Albania.

> The publication by the Bolshevik regime in November 1917 of the World War I secret treaties revealed that, according to the provisions of the April 1915 secret treaty of London, Albania was slated to be partitioned among Greece, Italy, Montenegro, and Serbia. This revelation served to intensify the efforts of Albanian activists to influence world public opinion. By early 1918 they had found a new ally in the president of the United States, Woodrow Wilson, . . . [who] was unequivocally opposed to the dismemberment of Albania. Owing mainly to Wilson's position on this issue, Albania emerged from the Paris peace conference (1920) with its independence and territorial integrity intact" (NP),

although Kosove was awarded to Serbia. That year, Albania was admitted to the League of Nations; in 1921, the Paris Conference of Ambassadors recognized Albania and the first Albanian elections were held. Several governments followed in rapid succession. In June, 1924, Fan S. Noli (1882–1965), the Orthodox Bishop of Durres, became Prime Minister after the previous government was deposed. Noli, Harvard educated, had been the Bishop of the Albanian Orthodox church in Boston before returning to Albania. He pledged to modernize the country and to implement a program of agrarian reform, but his government lasted only six months: powerful landed interests opposed his agrarian reform, his refusal to call elections disappointed many, and his foreign policy aroused alarm at home and abroad (especially his recognition of the Soviet Union). In December, the Noli government was overthrown by forces led by Ahmed Zogu (1895–1961), who had been Minister of the Interior in the previous government. Noli went into exile and eventually returned to the United States, where he served again as the Orthodox bishop in Boston, translated Shakespeare and other classics of Western literature into Albanian, and wrote a biography of Skanderbeg. He died in Boston and is buried there.

The Constituent Assembly declared Zogu President in 1925; in 1928 he crowned himself King Zog I. The strengths and weaknesses of the Zog regime continue to be debated (and at least one Albanian political party is dedicated to the restoration of the monarchy). Zog's return to power was partly supported by foreign interests(MV) and foreign investment was strongly encouraged during his reign (though his policies were inconsistent). "In 1929 and 1930 most of the Ghegs were making fire with flint and steel or with old-fashioned wick lighters," writes the anthropologist Carleton Coon.

> They did this slyly, and in my presence only when they could not borrow a match from me. King Zog had sold the match monopoly to the Swedish match trust, which had promptly set a price of five cents a box on penny matches. The king had at the same time prohibited the use of flint and steel or lighters. This left the mountaineers in an unenviable position – they could not afford matches nor legally start fires by other means.(CC)

For the first time, foreigners came to Albania in large numbers. Like visitors to Albania today, some of them were inspired to write about their experiences; at least two classics of the "sneering" genre of travel writing date from that era (see, for example, *Two Vagabonds in Albania*, and *King Zog's Albania*). Sympathetic observers noted that Zog built roads and now one could tour Albania by "motorcar." During Zog's regime, some of the dangerous malarial swamps were drained, and efforts were made to stamp out the blood feuds. The son of a *bajraktar*, Zog understood the power of the northern tribes all too well and sought to weaken it. But his achievements were offset by the ever-increasing penetration of Italy into every aspect of Albanian economic and political life. The country's vital statistics told a sad story: by the end of Zog's regime eighty five percent of the population was rural, the average life expectancy was thirty eight, and eighty percent of the population was illiterate(NP). Zog fled to Greece when Mussolini invaded Albania in 1939; he never returned to Albania, and died in Egypt. Today his son Leka is the pretender to the throne.

During World War II, Albania was occupied, at various times, by Italy and Germany. There was some cooperation on the part of prewar elites and the Catholic clergy and intelligentsia(NP), but for most Albanians national independence was paramount. There were two Albanian resistance movements, the communist Partisans (the National Liberation Movement), led by Enver Hoxha, and the anticommunist Balli Kombetar (the National Union); these groups fought not only the fascists but also each other. The Partisans were victorious, and proclaimed a provisional government in the south in 1944. They quickly established their rule throughout the country, and many supporters of the Balli Kombetar fled into exile. Outlawed during the communist era – only the communist Party of Labor was legal then – the Balli Kombetar is one of Albania's many political parties today.

The communist era. Writing recent history is always problematical; an objective account of the past fifty years in Albania, where the extremes and excesses of the communist regime are recent memory, is probably impossible. But everyone agrees on one thing: Albanian communism was not like the others.

> In the revisionist countries technocracy, along with – and as an expression of – bureaucracy, has become an important means whereby the working class has been deposed from leadership and capitalism has been restored . . . In our society we are following a diametrically opposite course. — Enver Hoxha(GM)
> Until his death in 1985, Enver Hoxha retained overwhelming personal dominance of the Party of Labour, the Communist Party, by a mixture of guile, terror and the intelligent use of placemen and southern Tosk ex-partisan loyalists from the wartime period. A cult of personality began to develop around Hoxha quite early on and by the mid-1960's had assumed overwhelming proportions, unparalleled in any communist country except Maoist China or North Korea under Kim Il Sung.(JP)

Once in power, the communists proceeded rapidly to implement their programs. In 1945 the landed estates were seized and given to the peasants, but soon the land was reclaimed for collectivization. Between 1945 and 1947, step by step, the private economic sector was eliminated. By the 1960's, the peasants were permitted neither garden plots nor animals. (A mountaineer told us how he had managed to keep an illegal pig. Hearing that an inspector would be visiting the next day, he plied the pig with brandy until it passed out, tied a kerchief on its head, and put the drunken animal under the covers. The inspector swallowed his story that the creature was his wife, sick in bed.)

The People's Republic of Albania was proclaimed in 1946. During the war and shortly afterwards, the Albanian communists worked closely with their Yugoslav counterparts, but relations soon cooled. In 1948, Albania broke relations with Yugoslavia; within a few years, it was closely allied with the Soviet bloc.

> "What appears to have finally confirmed Hoxha in his decision to align Albania totally with the Soviet Union was the existence, between 1949 and 1953, of a series of joint Anglo-American- sponsored clandestine operations intended to overthrow his government." These ventures failed because of poor planning and their betrayal to Moscow and Tirana by a Soviet agent within British intelligence, H.A. R. (Kim) Philby."(NP)

During the 1950's, though personal liberties were sharply curtailed, economic development was rapid: hydropower was harnessed, and timber, oil, nickel, coal, chromium and other resources began to be exploited. Albania was electrified – indeed, it exported electricity, and also agricultural products. Literacy and public health campaigns undertaken, and Albania's first university, the University of Tirane, was established in 1957, incorporating the Institute of Sciences, created in 1947. Within a decade, three hundred forty five thousand people had learned to read and write; by the end of the Hoxha era illiteracy had been eradicated, life expectancy was over seventy years, and there were sixty one thousand two hundred fifty six university or post secondary school graduates in the country, compared with three hundred eighty on the eve of World War II.(NP,HDR)

By 1956, the alliance with the Soviet Union had become strained, in part because Khrushchev had denounced the excesses of Stalin (whom Enver Hoxha had regarded as a friend of Albania), and in part because the Soviet concept of socialist division of labor would have required Albania to become a cog in the Soviet economic machine. In 1961, Albania broke relations with Soviet Union; after this momentous act, the country was isolated from the East Bloc as well as from the West.

But not yet from the Far East: beginning in the 1960's, and until 1978, Albania was closely allied with China. This brought some material benefits but repression took a sharp turn for the worse with the institution of an "Ideological and Cultural Revolution" in 1964. Although contemporaneous with the Chinese Cultural Revolution, Albania's seems to have been very much its own. After the break with China, Albania was truly alone. The economic sector deteriorated as it became impossible to buy new equipment or spare parts. The last remnants of idealism had long since vanished, people have told us, giving way to corruption and despair.

Enver Hoxha died in 1985. His successor, Ramiz Alia, pursued established policies for the most part, but instituted measures to ease – somewhat – the economic stresses that Albania's poverty and isolation had imposed on its citizens.

The Berlin wall came down in 1989, signalling the end of communism in Europe. Although to the outside world isolated Albania seemed untouched by the dramatic events taking place in other communist countries, internal pressures were beginning to build and small, hesitant, inadequate steps were being taken toward reform. But the measures were inadequate to meet the pent-up demand. Ismail Kadare's defection to France (1990) to protest the slow pace of change intensified pressures within the country. In 1990, freedom to practice religion was restored, and churches and mosques were reopened. The Hoxha era, if not the communist era, finally ended in 1991 when the students demolished the enormous statue – ten meters high – of Enver Hoxha in the center of Tirane.

Albania after 1991. And now? The (communist) Party of Labor won a majority of the seats in Parliament in the first democratic elections, in 1991, but mass destruction of public property and the collapse of industry and agriculture soon followed. Strikes ushered in a coalition government and new elections were held in 1992. This time, the Democratic Party, led by Sali Berisha, won overwhelmingly. A controversial land reform policy and shock therapy have been the basis for the Democrat's economic programs; it is too early to judge their long-term prospects for success, but for the short term the shock has been at least as great as the therapy. New judicial, educational, and other institutions are still evolving.

Songs Unsung

Deep within me sleep songs unsung,
Which neither suffering nor joy have yet brought forth,
Which sleep on awaiting a happier day
To burst out and be sung without fear or grief.

Deep within me my songs are dormant ...
I am a volcano, lying quiescent,
But when the day comes, they will all burst out,
In a thousand immortal colours spout.

But will the day come for my songs to awaken?
Or will the ages continue their derision?
No! no! Because freedom has begun to bloom
And I feel the warmth of the (allegoric) Sun.

Oh, sleeping songs, my personal relics,
Still to any other heart unknown.
Only I, like a child, with you am content,
I - your cradle, and perhaps your tomb.

Migjeni (1911-1938)

Reprinted with permission from *An Elusive
Eagle Soars; Anthology of Modern Albanian
Poetry*, edited and translated by Robert Elsie.
© UNESCO, 1993.

Opposite: *Katrina Lazri, Rragam.*

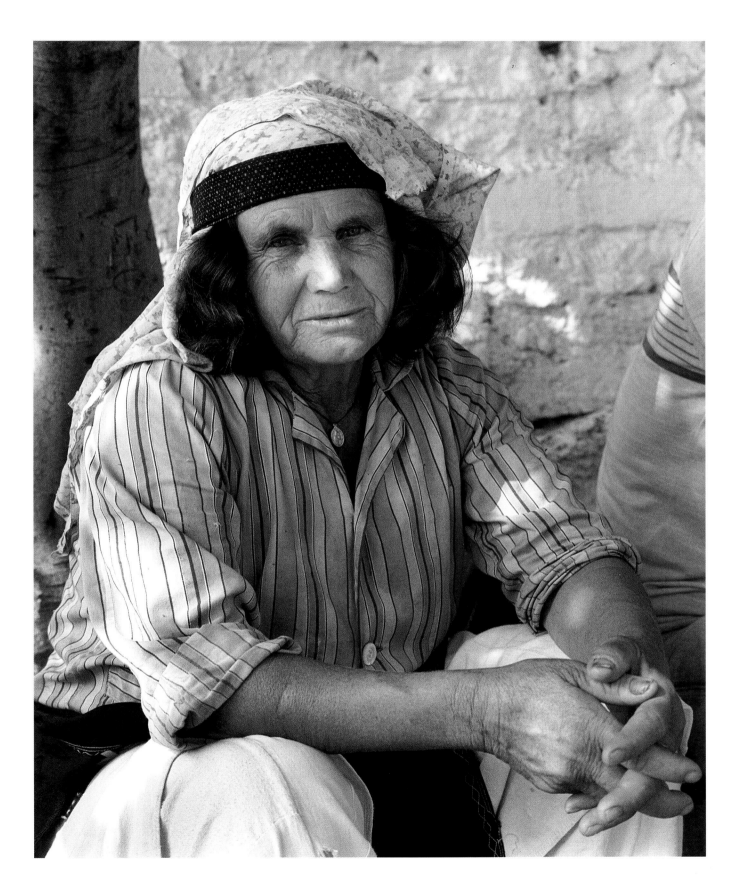

The Kanun of Lek Dukagjini

"For all their habits, laws, and customs, the people, as a rule, have but one explanation: "It is in the Canon of Lek" – the law that is said to have been laid down by the chieftain Leke Dukaghin . . . As for the laws and customs ascribed to him, the greater part are obviously far earlier than the fifteenth century, when he is said to have lived. They probably were obeyed by the unknown warriors of the bronze weapons in the prehistoric graves." — Edith Durham, *High Albania*

"All of these rituals which reinforce their social habits are of much greater importance to the Ghegs than the rites of church or mosque, which are not as well adjusted to this particular form of society. Another such mechanism is traditional law, codified and memorized as the Law of Lekë Dukagjin, which expresses the mountain attitude toward marriage and the selection of wives, and toward the blood feud. It serves to crystallize forms of behavior and inhibit change in those who are trained from childhood to believe in its infallible authority." — Carleton Coon, *The Mountains of Giants*

"The communists spent a good deal of time and energy in trying to stamp out the blood feud and revenge killings . . . in this they were following in the footsteps of King Zog pre-war, in his drive to integrate the northern tribes into the modern state . . . A principal target of communist propaganda among the peasants, particularly in the northern highlands, was the kanun of Lekë Dukagjin. Kanun is a word of Turkish origin, meaning legal code . . . With the end of communism there has been a marked revival of interest in the kanun, particularly in the north." — James Pettifer, *Albania (Blue Guide)*

"The Code of Lekë Dukagjini is a great cultural treasure, comparable to chapters of the Old Testament . . . It provides deep insights into the ancient society of the Albanians, their somber dignity and their magnificent sense of honor." — David Binder, *The New York Times*

"The "besa" or word of honor as stated in The Code of Lekë Dukagjini, which means peace and protection to those whom it is given, has become today an important fighting tool in the political struggle of Kosovo's Albanians against Serb oppression." — Victor Meier, *Frankfurter Allgemeine Zeitung*

Artist's conception of Lek Dukagjini holding a scroll of the kanun attributed to him. From Code of Lekë Dukagjini, *Gjonlekaj Publishing Company, 1989.*

LEK DUKAGJINI was a fifteenth century lord of a powerful northern family, a contemporary and comrade-at-arms of the celebrated Albanian hero Skanderbeg. In contrast to Skanderbeg, relatively little is known about Dukagjini, although the importance of his *kanun*, or code of customary law, for the history of Albania can hardly be overstated. "Skanderbeg" evokes the Albanian dream, "Dukagjini" the Albanian soul.

The edicts that Lek gathered into a *kanun* had been *de facto* law of the northern mountains from time immemorial, certainly for centuries, perhaps for millennia. No one knows the origins of this body of law; perhaps it has come down to us from the Bronze Age culture, as Edith Durham suggests. Some scholars maintain that the striking resemblances between the *kanun* and the Hindu *Laws of Manu* suggest a common source (there is some archaeological evidence to support the hypothesis that the earliest inhabitants of the Balkans came from India). And indeed, there are some obvious similarities between the *kanun* and the Laws of Manu, such as the veneration of the guest and the elaborate ceremony of a child's first haircut. But there the similarities end: if these two ancient codes had a common origin, they have evolved very differently, in keeping with the societies whose lives they guide. The *Laws of Manu* is mainly concerned with the behavior and duties of priests and kings; it is a foundation of the caste system. The *kanun* is concerned with the everyday life of ordinary people; priests are exempt from its laws, and the mountain people never have had kings. It is a remarkable document that enshrines the worst features of fifteenth century mountain society – and also the best.

Lek's *kanun* was not written down until early in this century; instead, it was passed on orally from generation to generation. Like any body of law, its application in particular cases was decided by a body of experts, and experts were certainly needed: the *kanun* deals with almost every aspect of social interaction. Among a myriad of other topics, it specifies every detail of weddings, the rights of inheritance, and the handling of animals. For example,

> The wedding ox must weigh 100 *oke* in meat and fat.
>
> A household without heirs passes to the cousins, who have equal rights; the property of the extinct house is divided among them in common.
>
> The chained dog is loosed after dinner [which is always after sun down] and remains free until dawn; when the sun rises, the dog must be found in his kennel with the chain around his neck.

Although it varies slightly from region to region, its essence is everywhere the same: the *kanun* is a formal expression of the elaborate and deeply felt concept of honor of the Albanian mountain people. Many seemingly arbitrary regulations in the *kanun* have their origins in the concern for honor, any offense to which must be avenged. "For example," writes Edith Durham, "a man told me that Lek had ordered that men should walk the length of one gun-barrel apart, lest in turning the barrel should accidentally strike the next man, for a blow even by chance must be avenged. And this law was to keep peace. Similarly women must walk the length of one distaff apart – they always spin on the march."

The *kanun* is specific about which offenses are to be punished (and how they are to be punished), for example,

> Plundering is avenged by plundering.
>
> Any damage, theft, or pilferage committed by children, petty thieves, and delinquents, if the perpetrators are discovered, must be paid for by the family to which they belong,

and which are to be avenged with blood:

If the guest has hung his rifle on a hook and the hook breaks, causing the rifle to fall on the ground, where it discharges and kills someone, the owner of the hook (i.e., the master of the house) incurs the blood feud.

The murderer may not dare to take the victim's weapon. If he commits such a dishonorable act, he incurs two blood feuds.

The *kanun* is specific about which offenses constitute dishonor:

A man is dishonored:

a) If someone calls him a liar in front of a group of men;

b) If someone spits at him, threatens him, pushes him, or strikes him;

c) If someone reneges on his promise of mediation or on his pledged word;

d) If his wife is insulted or if she runs off with someone;

e) If someone takes the weapons he carries on his shoulder or in his belt;

f) If someone violates his hospitality, insulting his friend or his worker;

g) If someone breaks into his house, his sheepfold, his silo, or his milk shed in his courtyard;

h) If someone does not repay a debt or obligation;

i) If someone removes the cover of a cooking pot in his hearth;

j) If someone dips a morsel of food before the guest, the guest is dishonored;

k) If someone disgraces the table in the presence of a guest, after the master of the house has had the dinner utensils removed.

And the *kanun* can be harsh:

An offense to honor is not paid for with property, but by the spilling of blood or by a magnanimous pardon (through the mediation of good friends).

The *kanun* is notorious because it codifies the epic blood feuds of these mountains. Too many accounts of the *kanun* dwell on this aspect alone, which is a serious distortion. But neither can it be ignored if one wants to understand Albania: the vendetta (revenge) is yet another theme of Albanian history that reverberates today. The *kanun* sets forth the offenses to honor under which blood feuds are incurred (thus becoming tragic burdens for the families involved) and the rules that govern their conduct. Unless a truce is declared, the feud must continue from generation to generation: once incurred, the original offense is itself irrelevant because now the honor of the family is at stake. Here are just a few of the many rules that must be obeyed by the participants:

The murderer, if he is able to do so himself, turns the victim over on his back. If he can, well and good; if not, he must tell the first person he meets to turn the victim over on his back and place his weapon near his head.

The relatives of the murderer must protect him during the first 24 hours after the killing because, if he is killed by someone from the victim's family, that person is simply avenging blood and does not incur punishment.

If the family of the victim has agreed to a truce with the murderer, the latter, even though he is the one responsible for the death, must go to the funeral and accompany the body to the cemetery, and attend the wake. This truce lasts for 24 hours.

These sad laws suggest that although the blood feuds were (and are) literally a matter of life and death, they are at the same time strangely impersonal, abstract tragedies performed on a lonely, majestic stage. Although forced to murder and be murdered in return, the actors entail no personal guilt – the blood feud is a collective concept involving the entire community. It can be ended only by a permanent truce which, like the feud itself, is declared through formalities:

> The "meal of the blood" occurs when the mediators of reconciliation of blood, together with some relatives, comrades, and friends of the "owner of the blood" go to the house of the murderer to reconcile the blood and eat a meal to observe that reconciliation.

> Two small glasses are taken and filled halfway with water or raki. Then one of the friends ties together the little fingers of the two parties and pricks them with a needle, causing a drop of blood from each to fall into the two glasses.

> After mixing their blood in this manner and stirring it well, the two men exchange glasses and, with arms linked, they hold the glasses to each other's lips, drinking each other's blood. Guns are fired in celebration and they become like new brothers, born of the same mother and father.

In the absence of a truce, the murderer is a marked man (in the past, the mark was literal: in some communities even during the truce he had to wear a black ribbon on his sleeve). He hides by day:

Refuge tower, Shale.

> The murderer may move around at night, but at the first sign of day he must conceal himself.

Marked men used to take refuge, by day, in special high, almost windowless, stone towers. Most of the towers are gone now, but we saw the one that still stands near Theth. It is a local curiosity, a museum. "No one uses the towers anymore," people explained to us. "These days we just go to another village." (Outlawed for decades by the communists, some feuding has resumed in recent years.)

Lek Dukagjini probably made things better, not worse, by bringing law and order into the lives of his countrymen through the detailed regulations of the *kanun*. But it was a very conservative order that put a premium on continuity,

> That which the ancestors decided with respect to the road may not be changed by later generations.

Thus it perpetuated the bad along with the good. Another regrettable aspect of the *kanun* is the life it prescribes for women. Like priests, women were exempted from the blood feuds (they did not have to kill, nor could they be killed; they lived on to mourn their husbands, sons, fathers, and brothers). But the *kanun* consigned women to very restricted roles, and did not allow them to own property or to have any say at all in the choice of a husband. According to the *kanun*,

> A woman is a sack, made to endure.

> To be married, according to the kanun, means to form a household, adding another family to the household, for the purpose of adding to the work force and increasing the number of children.

The young woman, even if her parents are not alive, does not have the right to concern herself about her own marriage; this right is held by her brothers or other relatives.

The girl who is betrothed may not reject the young man, even if she does not like him. If the girl refuses to submit to her fate under any circumstances, and her parents support her, she may never marry another man.

If her parents do not support her in this decision,

She should be handed over to him (her fiance) by force, together with a cartridge, and if the girl tries to flee, her husband may kill her with her parents' cartridge,

while on the other hand,

If the young man so desires, he is free to reject the young woman to whom he is engaged, but he loses the token (a ring) and all the money that has been given for the girl . . . both the young man and the girl are free to marry someone else.

Today a bullet is sometimes given to a bridegroom by his friends as a joke.

Although Albanian women have had full legal rights for decades, the *kanun*'s influence continues to be felt through the family structure that still forces many Albanian women into traditional roles.

Nevertheless, Albanian society is hardly the only one in which women have been oppressed, and blood feud traditions have existed in many countries, including the United States. A computer search on the subject heading "vendetta" in the holdings of the Harvard University Library shows these general categories:

VENDETTA —ARIZONA
VENDETTA —AUSTRIA —VORARLBERG —HISTORY —SOURCES
VENDETTA —BELGIUM —GHENT —HISTORY
VENDETTA —BIBLICAL TEACHING
VENDETTA —CROSS CULTURAL STUDIES
VENDETTA —FINLAND
VENDETTA —FRANCE —CORSICA
VENDETTA —FRANCE —CORSICA —HISTORY —19TH CENTURY
VENDETTA —FRANCE —CORSICA —PSYCHOLOGICAL ASPECTS
VENDETTA —GERMANY —GOTTINGEN —HISTORY
VENDETTA —GERMANY —HERFORD —HISTORY
VENDETTA —HISTORY
VENDETTA —ILLINOIS —WILLIAMSON COUNTY —HISTORY
VENDETTA —INDIA —ORISSA
VENDETTA —IRELAND —HISTORY
VENDETTA —ISRAEL
VENDETTA —ITALY —FRIULI —HISTORY —16TH CENTURY
VENDETTA —JAPAN —UTSUNOMIYA HAN
VENDETTA —KENTUCKY
VENDETTA —KENTUCKY —HISTORY
VENDETTA —MEXICO —OAXACA
VENDETTA —MEXICO —SINALOA STATE
VENDETTA —OMAN —HISTORY —20TH CENTURY
VENDETTA —PAKISTAN —THULL
VENDETTA —PERU —CUZCO —HISTORY —18TH CENTURY
VENDETTA —SCOTLAND —HISTORY
VENDETTA —SOLOMON ISLANDS —BELLONA ISLAND —CASE STUDIES
VENDETTA —SOUTHWEST NEW —HISTORY —19TH CENTURY
VENDETTA —SPAIN —MAJORCA —HISTORY

As a child growing up in Kentucky in the 1940's and 50's, I was raised on stories of the endless battles between the Hatfields and the McCoys; see under VENDETTA —KENTUCKY.

The *kanun* is important for modern Albania, not only because it shows what Albania has been, but also because it shows what it can be. There is another, much more positive side to the *kanun*, one that forms a solid basis for Albania's democratic aspirations. Although Albania was not a democracy under the Turks, or under King Zog, or under the communists, the *kanun* shows that Albanians have always known it, and have not forgotten it. Not only were there no kings in the mountains; no one ruled by virtue of his position alone.

> According to the Kanun, the control of the house belongs to the eldest living under the roof of the house or to his first brother. If he does not possess those qualities which are required to fulfill this office properly, then – on the basis of common consent – another member of the household is chosen, who is wiser, more intelligent, and more careful.
>
> The members of the household have the right:
>
> 1) To remove the head of the house if they see that he is not working for the benefit of the house and is leading it to destruction;
>
> 2) To remove the mistress of the house if it is noticed that she is stealing or selling anything in secret – even a single egg – or if she favors her own children over those of the others.
>
> The Elders are chosen from among the senior members of brotherhoods or from among the Chiefs of clans, and their functions support the foundation of legal rights.
>
> The blacksmith must not show personal favor, nor make distinctions between the rich and the poor or the distant and the close. His task is to attend to his customers by turns.

For men, at least, the *kanun* is profoundly egalitarian:

> In the kanun of the mountains of Albania, every male child born is considered to be good, and all are equal.
>
> Everyone considers himself good, and says to himself, "I am an honorable man," while he is greeted with the phrase, "Are you an honorable man?"
>
> If distinctions were made between the blood of one person and that of another, the law would not have an exact application and different standards based on individual character would be used with regard to pledges, but in fact, all men have the same value.
>
> If distinctions of blood were permitted, the ugly and the poor could be killed with impunity; murders would increase, since no one would be answerable for killing the ugly and the poor.
>
> For that reason, "Leka considered all blood equal; the good are born from the bad, and the bad from the good." "Soul for soul, God creates all."

The ancient tradition of the *besa*, or solemn oath, still unites Albanians, whatever their religious or regional differences, in their struggles for independence and liberty.

> The oath upon a rock, according to the kanun, is one of the most solemn and terrible oaths known to the Albanians of the mountains.

> The oath upon a "rock" is taken:
> a) to exculpate oneself from an accusation;
> b) to bind oneself by oath against intriguers and traitors to the country;
> c) to stand ready to confront common threats and dangers.

And the *kanun* also proclaims the magnificent tradition of mountain hospitality:

> The house of the Albanian belongs to God and the guest,

> At any time of the day or night, one must be ready to receive a guest with bread and salt and an open heart, with a fire, a log of wood, and a bed,

> If a guest enters your house, even though he may be in blood with you, you must say to him, "Welcome!"

> If someone mocks your guest or abuses him, you must defend your guest's honor, even if your own life is in danger.

Protection of the guest is celebrated in ancient epic ballads of the north. Marka Kuli, the hero of a song, pursued by the Turkish gendarmerie, arrived at the region of the three *bajraks*. When he asked the people what he ought to do, they replied that, as far as they were concerned, he was their guest and they would not deliver him:(SS2)

> The force of the king can take you,
> The law of the Mountains does not deliver you.

In another song an Albanian declares,

> I do not deliver my guest as long as I live.

Centuries later, during the Second World War, Albanians did not deliver their Jewish neighbors or guests to their Nazi occupiers. Throughout the country, Albanians hid and saved not only Albanian Jews, but also those fleeing from the fascists in Croatia and Greece; not one Jew was denounced. Those Albanian Rescuers whose stories are known have been honored by Yad Vashem in Israel and the Holocaust Museum in Washington, but many stories are still untold.

On a much more mundane level, we too were offered hospitality and protection everywhere we went in Albania, both in 1992 and in 1994. Complete strangers invited us to stay overnight, and our hosts of the moment always escorted us from their homes to wherever we were to go:

> The kanun therefore states that a guest should be accompanied because it is considered that he does not know the road and does not know whether he will encounter a friend or an enemy on it.

At no time did we ever feel unsafe, neither in the busy, crowded cities nor in the remote and isolated mountains.

As outsiders, many aspects of daily life, especially in the mountains, would have been puzzling to us if we had not been aware of the teachings of the *kanun*. Once, when I was seated in the kitchen of a mountain home after a long and difficult day, I saw that my hostess – a well-educated nurse who had grown up in Korçe – was heating a tub of water on the open hearth fire. Like all

Spinning wool, Lepushe.

houses in the northern mountains, this one had no running water, nor was there a modern stove; fetching the water, and then heating it, was heavy, time-consuming labor. I first supposed that the water was for a large soup; then, when nothing was added to it, I assumed it was for washing the dishes. But it turned out to be for my aching feet:

> A weary guest must be received and surrounded with honor. The feet of a guest are washed.

Another evening, in another mountain home, I noticed that the paths through cornfields we had been walking along during the day were now streams of rushing water:

> The village [irrigation] channel has its own branches.
>
> Water is taken from the branches toward sunset, according to the quantity to which a person is entitled: the full measure of the channel or a half or a quarter.

Even in Shkoder, where most people tend to scoff at it, the *kanun* makes its presence felt in countless ways, large and small. Few remember today why they accompany their guests on the road, or that it is the *kanun* that insists,

> No one may enter the house without giving notice of his presence in the courtyard,

although they still call out, probably with no idea of the source of the custom.

Several of the people you will meet in this book comment on the *kanun*; we leave further details to them.

The *kanun* of Lek Dukagjini, one of the world's great documents, is endlessly fascinating. Its influence on Albanian society can be – very loosely – compared to that of the Bible in Western culture, where the deeply religious, the casual believers, and agnostics and atheists alike use biblical metaphors and parables almost unconsciously. The variant of the *kanun* practiced in the Mirdite region (which differs only slightly from the variants practiced in the mountain regions we visited) was written down and edited early in this century by Shtjefën Konstantin Gjecov (1874–1929), a Catholic (Franciscan) priest. Gjecov's book was suppressed in Albania during the communist period, but copies of the *kanun* are sold in street kiosks in Shkoder today. Fortunately an excellent English translation is available in the United States; the quotations in this chapter are only a few of the one thousand two hundred sixty three recorded there. A broad picture of the inflexible role that the *kanun* played in the lives of the mountaineers in the 1930's is sketched in Ismail Kadare's poignant novel, *Broken April*, which is also available in English translation.

Contrasts

I have been begged by persons of these other [non-Macedonian Balkan] races to tell all that I have seen and heard . . . I have been begged by others not to tell all that I have seen and heard. It is impossible to please everyone. — Edith Durham, 1905

PAST AND PRESENT, ancient and modern, young and old, Muslim and Christian, rich and poor, north and south, urban and rural, monarchist and socialist: the extremes of Albanian society are vivid, its tensions palpable. But Albania is not "another Yugoslavia:" it is more like a tensegrity framework, a stable structure of rigid poles positioned in space – and linked together – by flexible cables. The cables are stressed but, barring catastrophe, they will not snap.

Like Edith Durham so many decades ago, we were begged to tell all that we had seen and heard: *tell our stories, the truth about our daily lives. Don't hide anything.* To these people we gave our word, and we have tried to keep it. The portrait of High Albania that we present in this book is as complete as we can make it within our serious limitations of time, background, and language.

We were also begged not to tell what we have seen and heard: *don' t show the world our poverty, our backwardness, our despair. Tell instead about the good things that are happening here, about our plans for the future, the natural beauty and richness of our land.*

Dear friends, your land is breathtakingly beautiful, your plans are shimmering with hope and determination, and thanks to your efforts many good things are indeed happening in Albania, things that would have seemed impossible only five short years ago. This is a large part of the story you tell in these pages. But you know as well as we do that to show only the positive would be false. Besides, no one is more critical of Albania society than you are yourselves. More than a few of you insisted to us that Albania is the worst place on earth and refused to believe us when we told you that it is not. When we explained that we have spent many months of our lives in even poorer places, in Africa, the Philippines, Russia, Brazil, New York City, and so we have some basis for comparison, you exclaimed: *but Albania is in the heart of Europe!* We' re not sure we agree with the way you see the map, but we think we understand what you mean. In the communist era you were taught that Albania was superior to all other nations; now you know that Albania is the poorest country in Europe. And it is also true that, as the old song says, nobody knows the trouble you' ve seen. But perhaps your long isolation has obscured the fact that other people too have suffered in our lifetime: the history of our sad century is a story of war, genocide, poverty, racism, famine, disease, all the evils that flew from Pandora' s box. Alas, although Albania' s history is different from everybody elas's its problems are not.

You may also find that some of the very things you consider poor and backward look very different to outside eyes, as they do to ours.

Opposite: *Sisters, near Shkoder.*

Above left: *Carrying brush, Rragam.*

Above right: *Carrying satellite dish, Shkoder.*

Above: *Kitchen, house in the village of Grizhe.*

Left: *Marije Alia in her kitchen, Bajze.*

Above: *Gjek Grishaj
sharpening his scythe, Lepushe.*

Right: *Gjovalin Kolombi, Rector of the
University of Shkoder, straightening
computer cable pins.*

Opposite page: *Bringing live sheep
from market, Shkoder.*

*Washing car in Lake
Shkoder.*

*Mothers and children
going home, Lepushe.*

43

CHAPTER TWO

MAY YOU LIVE ONE HUNDRED YEARS!

U bëfsh njëqind vjeç!

View of the Rozafa Castle, Shkoder.

In The Shadow of Rozafa Castle

YOU CAN SEE the high mountains from Shkoder, but most of the land nearby is flat. One magnificent exception is the high hill, a little south of town, on which stands the ancient Rozafa Castle. Two thousand years ago it was the site of an Illyrian fort; gradually it was extended until it became one of the great castles of the Balkans. The old stone road leading to the summit is still good, and it is not a long or difficult walk. Once there, on a clear day you can see not only the mountains to the north, but also the plains and villages to the south, the Buna River and Lake Shkoder to the west, and the rich farmland to the east. The famous Lead Mosque lies near the foot of the hill on the eastern side, while Gypsies have built homes up and down the western slope, above what once was the great Bazaar of Shkoder. The Bazaar was demolished by the communists, for the stated reason of draining the malarial swamp near which it stood.

The Bazaar of Shkoder, circa 1900.

National costume, Malesi e Madhe, circa 1900.

Men of Dukagjin, circa 1900.

The place is now a park in which several cafes have recently sprouted.

Every visitor to Shkoder visits Rozafa, but it is not yet a touristy place. In its small museum, you can see some of the castle's archeological treasures and learn something about its history, but on the castle grounds there are no signs explaining the great events that took place here over the course of two thousand years. The ramparts' disrepair invites the imagination. Which is the wall in which, according to the famous legend of the castle's construction, a young mother was immured alive? On which of these wild slopes was it that, after a ferocious battle in 1497, the corpses of sixty thousand Turks lay rotting under the scorching sun? Here the Albanian flag was raised in freedom in 1914; nearby, in 1991, demonstrators fought police and helped to usher in a democratic society.

Today, if history overwhelms you or the sunlight is too bright, you can go inside and have a soft drink in a charming cafe.

But Rozafa Castle is more than a place to visit, a place where you can learn something of the history of the ancient city of Shkoder. It is also a somber reminder that the shadows of the past are long here. The Albania being reconstructed today will be shaped, profoundly, by the events, customs, and attitudes of yesterday. Some of them are evident even to outsiders such as ourselves.

The ancient tradition of hospitality. The proper treatment of the guest is as much a matter of honor today as in the past. Visitors are surprised and touched by the genuine warmth with which they are invited into homes for coffee and *raki*, and often to stay overnight. The magnificent Albanian tradition of unconditional hospitality makes no distinctions among persons.

The ancient ways of mountain life. Life in High Albania's major city, its nearby villages, and the villages of the remote mountains is a closely knit fabric of kinship and memory. In some deep pockets of the mountains, life has not changed very much in some respects in hundreds of years, while other mountain villages blend the old and the new. Many families living in or near Shkoder today are mountaineers or descendents of mountaineers who left their impoverished communities in search of a better life. Mountain culture, with its emphasis on personal and family honor, the oath, or *besa*, and the pervasive *kanun*, frames contemporary city life just as the mountains frame the city landscape.

The effects of Ottoman occupation. The casual visitor today finds only three very obvious traces of the 500 year Ottoman occupation – graceful mosques, the splendid 18th century Mes Bridge, and a very strong preference for very strong Turkish coffee. If you study the Albanian language, you will find some words of Turkish origin, but Albanian has borrowed words from French, Latin and other languages as well. Through the 1920's, Turkish influence was obvious in the clothes worn by women in the streets of Shkoder, but now you have to visit an antique dealer in order to see such garments. Nevertheless the effects of the long occupation were deep. To give only one example, until this century most schools were taught in Turkish. There was no university in the entire country until after the Second World War; until then, the best students were sent abroad for their university educations. Today, the University of Tirane is the largest and most important university in the country, but several pedagogical institutes, including the one in Shkoder, have recently been upgraded to university status and are rapidly expanding.

The tradition of religious tolerance. Today's fast-paced reconstruction of churches and mosques might seem to suggest a rivalry between the Catholic and Muslim communities of Shkoder, but traditionally religious differences have not mattered much here. Albania has often been cited as a model of tolerance, although some observers suggest that this tolerance may be due in part to a relative indifference to religion. Nevertheless, the two communities are clearly distinct in Shkoder, despite many friendships between individuals (for example, Catholics and Muslims rarely intermarry). There have also been some cultural tensions. Will tolerance continue to prevail?

The traditional family structure. As elsewhere in the Balkans and indeed in many parts of the world, it is has long been the custom in Albania for brides to live with their husbands' families. In some cases, the result is a pleasant, cooperative, extended family, but in others, the young bride becomes the servant of the older members of the household. (An amusing Albanian film, *A Tale From the Past*, tells the story of a young woman who is married off to a fourteen year old boy because his mother needs a worker and her family has too many mouths to feed.) Traditionally, the marriage was arranged by the couple's parents; the bride may not have met her husband-to-be before the engagement. Today this has changed, of course, but families still play a strong role in their children's choices.

Perhaps this is the place to retell the ancient Rozafa legend. It has many variations, but the gist of it is always the same. When the castle was being built, each night evil spirits undid the work that had been done during the day. The builders, three brothers, consulted a soothsayer who told them that to appease the evil spirits one of their wives must be bricked up inside the wall. By chance or design, the victim turned out to be the wife of the youngest brother. Heroically, she accepted her fate, but as the wall grew higher around her, she begged them to leave an opening through which she could continue to nurse her infant son. Her request was honored, and to this day there is a damp milky-white spot in that very place on the castle wall (though no one can show you exactly where it is).

*Mes Bridge,
1994.*

Different authors have treated the Rozafa legend in various ways. It is the subject of Marguerite Yourcenar's tale *Le Lait de la Mort (The Milk of Death);* she recounts a Serbian version of the legend. The Albanian version is retold in Ismail Kadare's novel *The Bridge of Three Arches.* In Kadare's rendition, a monk, circa 1377, tells the story to a visitor who then picks it apart, trying to make sense of every detail. Why did this young woman accept her fate so calmly, he wonders, and then suggests, "The youngest wife agreed to be sacrificed, because her sisters-in-law and her mother-in-law had made life impossible for her . . . She preferred death to that living hell."

Most of the young women we met accepted the traditional living arrangement as a fact of marriage, and assumed that their only choice was between that and no marriage at all.

The legacy of fifty years of Europe's most draconian communism. This is the darkest shadow of the past, a past that ended only in 1991. It affected the lives of everyone; they will tell you about it in their own words.

As the older people whom you will meet in this chapter speak about the past, they speak about the present and future as well.

Faces and Voices
the echoing past

MY NAME IS RROK MARKU, I am ninety years old. I have known many things, but now I have started to forget, because the burden of the years is great. We have had a very difficult life. We are from Kelmend, near Vermosh, at the border with Yugoslavia. In 1912, we came here to Grizhe. At that time my grandfather had six children and life was very difficult – they lived amidst rocks over there. We have had a very good time here, with friends and so on. We have lived those times that were not modern times like now. We were wealthy and healthy. We used to have two hundred fifty to three hundred animals: sheep, cows, horses. People now have cars, but at that time we used horses. I can't complain, it is good now too, but we were used to the land, to the animals, to wealth, to manhood, not to insult anybody. We had much better relations with one another at that time. We loved one another. We used to say, "Where is this America?" And the answer was, "In my land." We didn't know where other kingdoms were, because we didn't move from our place.

What happened to your land?

There is trouble with the land now. There are a lot of quarrels about that.

We mean, what happened when the land was collectivized?

I don't hear well. Oh, they took everyone's, and they forced everyone to join the cooperative, and they told us that you have nothing to do with the land anymore, and from now on it is we who are going to take care of you with seven hundred grams of bread. And they allowed us to keep only five chickens. If we had more chickens, we had to keep them secretly, because they were considered dangerous to the wheat. Cows were allowed only in the most remote mountainous villages. They have destroyed almost everything here, the land and the livestock. But we have to speak the truth, the total truth. They were good in one respect, they didn't let people kill one another [in bloodfeuds]. As for the other things, they were very severe, very severe. Imagine, going and buying bread produced on your own land!

Opposite: *Rrok Marku holding flute, Grizhe.*

MY NAME IS LUIGJ FRANJA; I was born in 1916. I finished high school in Shkoder and then continued my studies at the University of Padua, Italy, for four years. I taught the Albanian language and Italian, and also some Latin. Then I did scientific research on the influence of Latin on the lexicology of the Albanian language. According to the *Vocabulary of the Albanian Language* of 1962, there are six hundred Latin words in Albanian. I was able to double this number; I discovered over 600 other words. I have also sent some articles on the infinitive of Albanian verbs for publication. I also studied in the field of history, on the revolt of Haxhi Qamili in 1914. I worked as a teacher in Elbasan, in Durres, in Gjirokaster, and in Prishtine, Kosove, where I left a part of my heart.

I have tried to work honestly and conscientiously all my life. As far as I know, I never made any mistakes in my job. But the material and moral rewards have been almost nonexistent. And now, when I am reaching the end of my life, I keep asking myself *quo vadis?* Life is different for everybody. Some have a good life, others do not. Some are rich and others are poor. Not all the fingers of the hand are of the same size. One is small, another is large. I remember *Les Misérables* of Victor Hugo. Its hero, Jean Valjean, is put in jail for a long time because he tries to steal a crust of bread, while others, who steal in millions, are given medals. This is the irony and the tragicomedy of life.

MY NAME IS ARTA FRANJA; Arta is the name of a city in Çameria, where my father fought against the Greek *andarts*. That's why he wanted to name me Arta. I am a native of Korçe, and my parents, both of them, were teachers in elementary schools. So, when I was just a little girl I wanted to be become a teacher too. And that was realized. I did my secondary studies in Albania. I think that my school had connections with someone in America, because both the director and the vice director had lived in America. I learned English from American and English teachers. In '33 it was closed, that institution, and I had no more English. I was a little bit privileged: my parents wanted me to study outside [abroad] because here in Albania there were no higher institutions or universities, for boys or for girls. So after I finished my studies in the gymnasium, I went to Italy for four years to study mathematics and physics. My parents asked me in each letter how I was doing with my studies. And I was proud of my country; I didn't want people to say that Albanians are not able to continue higher studies. For both reasons I studied hard. After I graduated, I came here to Scutari as a teacher. I have been teaching mathematics, physics, and astronomy in Scutari all my life, except for four years when I was in Gjirokaster. I have worked very very hard. I listened to my students' problems, their troubles, and their joys and their successes too, and I have many friends now who were my pupils before. I am very happy and glad to see them grow up and go forward in their lives.

Opposite: *Luigj and Arta Franja in their one room apartment, Shkoder.*

Nusha Fistani in her
apartment, Shkoder.

MY NAME IS NUSHA FISTANI, my maiden name was Zeka. I was born in 1910. In 1925 I was a member of the first graduating class of the high school for women in Shkoder. I have a diploma, too. It was the first time that such a thing had happened in Shkoder; the first school in Albania for women was in Korçe. Nine girls graduated; I have a picture of that class, it is there, behind you. After that I went to the pedagogical school. All our teachers were nuns, sisters, and they had all studied in Italy, or in France – one taught us French. There was also Father Anton Harapi, who taught us pedagogy. And also Father Martin Gjoka who taught geography, history and music. We received a broad Western culture from them. When the communists came to power, they closed the school and they dispersed all the people who were teaching in it. They destroyed everything.

It was in 1928 that I graduated from the pedagogical school. Right after that, I was appointed as a teacher in Durres. I also worked in Kavaje for two years. All in all I spent seven years there before returning to Shkoder. I was the principal of the schools both in Durres and in Kavaje. I was also appointed principal in Shkodra, at the school named Xhamija e Vogel (The Small Mosque), whose name I later changed to Teuta. I worked at this school as a principal until the liberation of Albania. When the communists came to power, they offered me the chance to remain the principal of the school, but I resigned. I have also worked in other schools in Shkoder; I retired in 1960. Can you please close that door? I think there is a stream of air.

What were the conditions in the schools where you were teaching? Did you have enough books?

They still don't have books. But it's not for books that they are suffering now. In my time I had a lot of books.

In the days before the communists, in the twenties, thirties, and forties, were many women working in professions in Shkoder?

There were a few women who went to school. But many others, those whose families came from the mountains, used to cover their faces with veils, and they stayed at home. I loved to go to school, and I also had a talent for it. All those other women in that picture are rich. They went to school because they liked it, it was just a pleasure for them. Three of them didn't work after they graduated – Terezina Shehu, the sister of Doctor Shiroka, Liza Kodheli, the daughter of Kel Marubi, and another one I don't recall now. I had to work as soon as I graduated. They didn't pay much attention to me at school, because I was a poor girl. While the rich people used to send presents, expensive presents, to the school – I remember Terezina Shiroka sending grapes, large baskets of grapes. Also at that time Father Vincent Prenushi, the Archbishop of Shkoder, was a kind of tutor at our school. He used to go to the Ministry of Education to resolve many of the school's problems. He looked out for each of us. I still have a letter from him, where he tells me, "I have taken care of you and another student. And I have heard so many good words about you." Also Father Gjergj Fishta looked after me and helped me a lot. He used to tell us that they boasted about us.

I first saw the fascists who occupied Albania close to the house of the Gurakuqi family. I went out there, at Frater's street, and I saw some Italian Fascists. I started crying when I saw the fascists marching in our streets. They were so many. When the Germans occupied Shkoder, they used to march in front of our school with automatic guns, pam-pam-pam. Like dogs. In that street, in front of my school, called Ndre Mjeda at that time, when the post office was still there. We were afraid to look at them.

We have suffered a lot. However badly you might be treated by your own people, it is better than the foreigners coming and occupying the country.

MY NAME IS HAJRIE BAJRAM CURRI. I was born in Gjakove, in Kosove. The Serbs were prepared to pay anyone who could find the wife of Bajram Curri. When I was a little child my family used to cover my mouth with a piece of cloth so no one would be able to hear my screams. We crossed the border illegally and found a way to come to Shkoder. I lived with my father for only a very short time. But even in those few years, he was away from home most of the time – abroad, in Tirane, in the mountains. He was involved in many activities, for the good of Albania. I didn't have the chance to grow up with that father, who was a very good father for others.

All the important people of Shkoder, the highly educated ones, said to us, "You should be proud of your father because he is a great man and you are respected people." In Shkoder and all over Albania we were accorded a great deal of respect all the time. I was raised in that climate, but all the time in the absence of my father. We lived fifteen years during the period of King Zog. My mother, concerned and upset and disappointed because her husband had been killed, did not accept a pension for two years, because King Zog refused to admit that he was responsible for my father's death. He was anxious and sent many ministers to the house of the Curris to say, "I cannot sleep; please accept this pension. Why don't you accept my pension?"

We went to Italy and there we met many Albanian immigrants. They said, "You have lost your husband, you have children to raise, why didn't you accept the pension? It is not King Zog's pension. It is the pension given by the people of Albania because your husband fought for his country – and you should accept it." Only then did my mother agree. It was eighteen ducats, in gold. Zog wanted to assuage his guilty feelings.

I grew up, became a young woman ready for my wedding, I was married. I had a sister. When we came back to Kosovo for the first time, for two weeks, my sister died. It was very upsetting for us – a disappointment for all of our family.

During the communist period I suffered again. My husband was in jail for seventeen years. At that time I was alone with my mother and my children – two women alone – and the people of the communist regime created many troubles for us – singing songs to our family, knocking at the door in the middle of the night, and making us afraid.

I have two daughters. I gave them a good education. They were models of honesty, and very good in sports, gymnastics. But they were not treated very well. In such conditions, they lost the will to improve themselves because they were treated as second class. Nevertheless, they finished college. But I suffered raising my daughters in such circumstances. I didn't even have enough food for my family. There were coupons for bread – for one hundred grams of bread for each person, but we were denied even these. Only a person by the surname Barli, in Tirane, raised his voice and said, "how is it possible that the daughter of Bajram Curri, the Albanian hero, does not have bread coupons?" When we got the coupons, my two daughters kissed them. When I remember this I start to cry. I am not capable of telling more.

Opposite: *Hajrije Bajram Curri, her husband Ragip Meta, and portrait of her father, Bajram Curri.*

The Myftia family, Shkoder.

MY NAME IS XHEVDET MYFTIA. I am eighty years old. I came from a rich family. My great-grandfather was a Grand Mufti. My grandfather was a Grand Mufti, too. And also my father. We owned property before the war. We had a water mill in Vroke and life was very good for us. I went to Italy, to Yugoslavia; my only aim in life was to dress well and to visit other countries. Then, after the communists came to power, they took our properties away, the land, the shop and everything we had. The communist regime offered me only the most difficult work, for very little money. I didn't work before communists came to power. I was the landlord of the fields around here. We had 400 acres. Now we are dreaming of taking them back.

I AM SADETE MYFTIA, I am sixty four years old. After I finished elementary school I had to stay home because that's what women were supposed to do at that time. We had to stay covered and we weren't allowed to go out. My father was a great industrialist and we didn't need to work. We used to stay home and embroider. When I was eighteen, I was engaged to be married.

After I was married we went to Tirane to visit some friends of ours. But then I had to stay home because we were rich and we didn't need to work. Our life was wonderful at that time. We had enough money to eat well, dress well and go anywhere we liked to. We lacked nothing. We went to the movies and other places. Then, after the communists came here, they took everything we had and we had to start working. I made baskets. I had to carry the sticks with which I made them. My children helped me. It was such hard work that I sometimes wonder how I am still alive today.

We continued to live in this house, but we had to share half of it with other people. They were here until recently. No one can remember how old the house is. It was built by the great-grand father. It was improved time after time; every generation did something to improve it. But later, as many people lived in it, it got damaged.

MY NAME IS LORENC VATA. I was born in Shkoder in October, 1920, and I was educated in a Franciscan religious school here. I was a good chess player and I participated in the first championship in Tirane. When I came back to Shkoder, I was arrested and put in jail. During the investigations, I was accused of having had contacts in Tirane with people who were thought to be bad. I told them that they should read a sports newspaper. But even after reading it and verifying that I had been at a chess championship, they proceeded with their accusation. Then I went to trial. It was a military trial, without a lawyer to defend me, and without any other kind of support, like human rights organizations. I spent seventeen months in the process of investigation. Sometimes I was treated badly. I was sentenced to life in prison. I moved from one jail to another, all over the prisons of Albania – in Shkoder, in Korçe, in Beden, and so forth. When I was released, I got a job as a dock worker. I worked in many different factories in Shkoder. But many times I was suspended and quite often I was fired from my job. Every time I faced new difficulties and each time I had to work in new, difficult jobs – preparing bricks, digging ditches, working on heavy things all the time. In order to survive this situation, I started to develop a hobby

for antiques, something I had dealt with since I was a young man. I was afraid to speak with other people here, because I was under too much pressure. As soon as I started communicating with someone, the *Sigurimi* [the secret police] would come and ask me "What were you talking about?" To avoid this, I devoted all my time and my thoughts to archeological findings and things like that. Now, after thirty seven years of work, I am retired. I receive a pension, which is about twenty six dollars per month. Now I still devote my time to antiques, antiquities and such things in order to survive.

Right: *Antiquities such as this Shkodran dress, circa 1900, are sold in Shkoder by Lorenc Vata and other antiquarians.*

Opposite: *Lorenc Vata preparing coffee, Shkoder.*

MY NAME IS ROBERT ASHTA. I was in born in 1918 and when I was ten years old I went to the Franciscan seminary. I finished high school here in Albania and then I went to theological school in Italy. When I came back to Albania I worked in different churches. During this time I was in the military service for twenty seven months and I had a red star on my cap. Later I worked in villages as a priest. One of them was divided in two parts, the lower village and the upper village. In the upper part there were eight or ten Catholic families, and two or three hundred Muslims in the lower. Muslims and Catholics celebrated the Feast of Saint Mary on the fifteenth of August, together. And they sacrificed sheep and celebrated St. Nicholas together, both of them. The church was destroyed. After twenty years I went there to celebrate the first mass. All the Catholics came there and also three hundred Muslims, with their *hoxha*. The people and the chief of the commune were Muslims, and all of them want to rebuild the church there. The Muslims brought water, they washed their faces and hands, and all said that they had found miracles of St. Mary . . . nobody knows this. I wanted to return to that church but I was sent to Dukagjin. May God help them to rebuild the church.

I was also in Tropoje for two years, and in Vukil for twelve years. Sometime when I was walking to people who were sick, I got stuck in the snow. We kept an axe and ropes with us for the ice. There was no road there before the churches were closed, neither in Vermosh nor in Dukagjin.

The missionaries taught people all of the Catholic catechism – *pater noster, ave maria, gloria patrii*, the sacraments, the penitence – as a song, a poem. And in this way they remembered everything. They have been singing it since old times, since the time of the Turks, because they have kept Catholicism in those mountains. When the churches were closed, I was in Vukil. When the communists came to close them, I said to them I won't close the church until I ring the bell so all the people will come here together. I rang the bell, and people came to the church. I blessed five kilograms of water, to use it for holy water, and I heard the confessions of all the people who were there and I gave communion to all of them. People cried. And then the two policemen took everything that was in the church. They left me only with a pair of clothes, not with these but with lay clothes, and I walked two days to Shkoder. They kept all the books; they didn't leave anything.

But now something extraordinary has happened: the Pope made me an archbishop when I was seventy five years old!

Dukagjini, which is my diocese, is a very difficult district. When I went there for the first time, I stayed there for nine months, and I was the only priest there. There was no church and no house to live in. Now they have bought a house prefabricated in Italy – it is already finished – and I want to go there to live because here I am out of my diocese. My center will be in Gjan. There is an old cathedral there. The diocese of Dukagjin has been known for eight hundred years, maybe eleven hundred years. The people fought the Serbs and the Turks. It is an interesting fact that they were always with the Pope of Rome. They are very very poor, much worse than Lepushe or Vermosh. They have no land, they have few animals, and they have continued fighting and fighting in the mountains, for blood revenge. The Turks couldn't enter that district. Everyone had to solve their problems by the law of the mountains.

The worst thing for us is that the government doesn't take care of Dukagjin. It doesn't take us into consideration, they don't give us our rights. We have democracy but we don't know where this democracy is. The ex-communists now live in houses that were churches before, and they won't give them up to be used as churches again. The windows of the schools are without glass; they haven't tables and they haven't chairs. The schools are just like caves, and the teachers don't teach, even foreign languages are not taught there. I have proposed that they study English and German but they have done nothing. They are very intelligent, but they are looking only into darkness.

*Archbishop Robert
Ashta in his study,
Shkoder.*

*Gjon Shllaku at his
writing table, Shkoder.*

MY NAME IS GJON SHLLAKU. I'm seventy two. When I was sixteen years old I studied in a Jesuit Seminary. There I graduated from the Classical Liceum. I studied philosophy for three years and I was studying in the third year of theology, just about to become a priest, when I was jailed. I was twenty two years old at that time and I spent eleven years in prison.

We were raised in hardship. The best years of my life were the ten years I spent at the Seminary, from 1935 to 1945. These were the only years that I remember during which I have done what I liked to do in life. I am very grateful to them. The Seminary was one of the best schools of Europe at that time. There is a story about a man who was working on a palace, making some repairs. It happened that a brick slipped from his hands and fell on his head. He started bleeding, and was taken to the hospital. Something affected his brain: right after that he turned into a real genius. If it wasn't for that Seminary, who knows what I would have become. I wouldn't have been an educated person.

When I was young I translated selected classics of Latin literature, Virgil and Lucretius. Later I translated from French and from ancient Greek literature, especially Homer. I had studied ancient Greek for five years at school, and also Latin for eight years. Philosophy and theology were both taught in Latin, as Latin was the language of the clergy. There were no other foreign languages taught there. While a student I read most of the works of the Greek classics, of Sophocles, Aeschylus and Euripides, because I had made up my mind to dedicate part of my time to Greek literature. And I succeeded. I followed a well-thought-out plan, which I had envisioned when I was very young. In jail I kept studying all the time and I also translated parts of the Bible – the Apostles and the Saints. I translated from Greek, intending to go deeper and deeper into the language. When I was in jail, I came across a very good anthology of Homer's works and I promptly translated it all.

It was in jail that I learned modern Greek, which has been very useful for me. It served me when I was in Greece as part of a delegation. I have spoken at different conferences, I have delivered some speeches and I have given interviews for Greek TV. In jail I learned Spanish and some English, too. I can read English easily. I want to learn much more English, but I have other work to do and time is so short. You can't hold two watermelons under one arm.

Up to now, the *Iliad* of Homer has been published in Albanian in two versions, in the Gheg dialect and in the Tosk dialect. Other manuscripts that I had sent to the Naim Frasheri Publishing House were never published because I was a persecuted person at that time. I was able to get my manuscripts back only two years ago. Now I have a new project which makes me happy and which will be very helpful for the Albanians, too. As the works of Sophocles and Euripides are part of the Greek literature, the Greek Embassy has offered to sponsor my translation of these works. The Soros Foundation, too, has been ready to help with their publication. They have done the editing work with them, I have been paid for it, and they will surely appear in print by August or September. I have another chance to work on Virgil, and I have applied to the Italian Embassy for support. I had the opportunity to meet the Italian Ambassador. He told me that they had received my letter and that they were going to do something about it. So, just like the young Greeks who were interested in the fate of the wars of the old Greeks, the Italians are going to be interested in the Georgics, who are the descendants of the Latins. So one of my wishes is fulfilled and I hope to see all of them realized before dying, if God helps me. I work very intensively. This is a short description of my life.

*Marije Palndoçi at her
sewing machine, Gajtan.*

MY NAME IS MARIJE PALNDOÇI; I am seventy two years old and I live here in Gajtan. When I was young there were a lot of older people in this house, six of them. I was obliged to live here because I married into the family. It was not easy for me; I had to live quite differently from that time on. I accepted many hardships in order to be able to maintain the tradition of the family and keep it alive. We have a word in Albanian: *korit*, which means dishonor. "You saved me from dishonor," my husband told me, "because you have agreed to live with the old people and serve them, which is not an easy task to do." I suffered a lot raising nine children. I have to kneel down and kiss the earth because I have been rewarded by God. My seven daughters are married and live with honor. No one can speak ill of them and I am so grateful for that. It is for that reason that I am ready to kiss the earth.

Albanians prefer to have sons instead of daughters. I had seven daughters. I prayed to God to have a son. After twenty three years of marriage I was able to have my first son, but he died. Later I had three other sons.

I am seventy two years old but I'm still strong. I used to go to the mountain to get wood, and I carried the load on my back. Once my husband told me to stay home because he was going to take care of the wood. He told me to prepare *raki* from the mulberry.

Why don't you all come inside. Please, do come and have some rest, drink coffee and then eat something. When my son's bride comes, she will prepare food for us.

MY NAME IS MARASH NOU. I am from Lekaj, Dukagjin. I'm sixty eight years old. I am a *rapsod*. I started playing the *çiftelia* when I was ten years old. I play both the *çiftelia* and the *lahute* at weddings, feasts, and festivals. I've been in the Festival of Gjirokaster three times. And I'm playing for you.

The Old Lahuta

The lahuta rests in silence on a beam,
for their uncle died some time ago
and his nephews cannot play it.
The lahuta rests in silence in the smoke,
its fretboard broken
like the uncle's fingers now.
The nephews still hear the lahuta's story,
strong and manly at the hearth
with the old song
fading away in the chimney.
And the carved snake moves in time
to the tremor of the uncle's voice
and the steed-mounted heroes with swords
fly over the snakeskin sounding-board.

The lahuta rests in silence on a beam,
like the uncle's fingers now,
but in the nephews' soul remains
a sound for the new song.

Martin Camaj (1925-1992)

Reprinted with permission from *Martin Camaj: Selected Poetry,* translated by Leonard Fox.© New York University Press, 1990.

Opposite: *Marash Nou playing the* lahute, *Shale, Dukagjin.*

MY NAME IS ANGELIN NENSHATI. I worked as a photographer and that was the most difficult part of my life, because of the lack of freedom. We didn't worry about economic poverty as much as we worried about the lack of freedom of expression, or the lack of freedom to do things as we wanted to do them. I have always made photos. But I have never been free. We were always told what to do. There is a photo montage through which I tried to describe the life of the Albanian people. The theme was, "We are building socialism with a rifle in one hand and a pickaxe in the other." We had to work hard with the pickaxe in order to build socialism, and to fight with the rifle to protect our country from the capitalists and revisionists surrounding us. We couldn't create anything. We were exploited, as if we were merely tools. And it was the government that profited from us and our work. It was also a war against the Roman Catholic religion. All the people that were jailed were educated people, writers, poets, who had studied in the best universities of Europe. That is why they are considered Martyrs of Democracy.

This is a picture of Shkoder. It was made purposefully, shot in a way that would make Professor Arshi Pipa miss this city less. Since 1945 this city has passed through a real hell of sufferings. The city was the target of the communist attack. Enver Hoxha's motto was to fight any form of reaction against the regime. As you can see in this picture, there is a slogan saying "Let's fight against the reaction." The consequences of this fight were massacres, poverty, church destructions, and a whole people left in such a miserable state that they didn't have enough to feed themselves. And also a lot of trials, executions of people they considered "traitors." The so-called traitors were people like Preng Cali, who defended the Albanian borders, Dom Ndre Zadeja, a poet, and Ndoc Jakova, the head of the Roman Catholic faith in this country. He was killed when he was twenty five. This woman, look at this picture over here, is a symbol because when her husband went to fight against the communists, she said "I am not going to leave you alone" and she followed him and they were both killed. Don Lazer Shantoja, a priest who had served in Switzerland. Myzafer Pipa, the brother of Arshi Pipa, who was a lawyer. He was sentenced because he defended a priest in court. All the others are writers. This young man was executed because his brother had escaped from the country. At that time, Arshi Pipa was in jail, too. This man here, the Archbishop, Monsignor priest Vincent Prenushi, priest of Durres and Monsegnor of Vlore, died before his eyes. All these prisoners spent more than thirty years in prison. Those here were in jail for twenty three, twelve, twenty five, twenty two, twenty eight years. The one with twenty eight years is now the Speaker of the Albanian Parliament. The priest who opened the first church was sentenced for twenty six years. Monsignor Koliqi, who is now ninety three years old, spent thirty eight years in prison.

Today everyone can do anything he likes. That's why you can now see pictures that I wouldn't have dared to take before.

Angelin Nenshati in his
kitchen darkroom, Shkoder.

M Y NAME IS ZEF GRISHAJ. I was born in February, 1938, in Vukil, a village about fourteen kilometers from here. I have lived here in Lepushe for twenty five years. In my childhood I was fond of stock breeding, especially goats. Later I got the idea of going to school. At that time, although the school was there, we preferred to become shepherds, instead of students. When I was about seventeen years old, I went to Shkoder for a one month course and from that time on I continued studying. When I was in the army, I spent all my free time reading books and studying different things. I have been studying continuously from 1958 to the 1990's and I worked at the same time. I was a soldier from 1958 to 1960, and from 1960 to 1962 I studied at a professional school for the wood industry. And from the 1960's to the 1990's I worked as a wood and pasture technician.

I was very fond of my profession; I worked as a forest guard, protecting the trees from damage. I used measuring tools, for example for measuring the height and the circumference of the trees. So I dealt for twenty five years with the damages, the production and the protection of the forests. During the last five years I mainly dealt with pastures. I had to protect about four thousand years hectares. There were two economic areas. One, "The Vermoshi Valley," had three thousand nine hundred hectares and the other, "The Meadow of the Bear," about one thousand hectares. This last one is bordered north and east by ex-Yugoslavia. The first one is bordered in the South by Selce, while in the north it is bordered by Montenegro.

I was the only one who worked in the area. But the law was very strict then. I traveled mainly by foot. I kept working until I was convinced that everything was okay. That was all we could do in those times. We didn't have other entertainment, traveling or anything like that. We were pleased to give all our effort just to provide the daily bread. Now there are a lot more pleasures in life. People are free to go everywhere they want to go.

To do your work well you have to live close to it. My family lived in Vukil, three hours away from here. So I decided to be as close to my work as possible, and we moved here. There was no private property at that time. We found here the same things we had left behind. We just moved from one cooperative to another and it cost us nothing. We came on foot. It was easy. We had to carry our belongings on our backs, as well as our two kids.

At that time there were very few houses in Lepushe. First I had to move into a summer house, a sort of large umbrella. And then I built a very small house that was just better than being outside in the open. I stayed there for fifteen years, from 1969 to 1984. It was somewhat difficult, but the house was very small and we had enough fire to warm it. And we were not too many people at that time, just four of us. It wasn't that bad. In 1984 I moved to the new house, which took me eleven years to build.

When the communist period ended, each family had to privatize the land around their house. There were meetings in the villages to decide how to divide the land.

Opposite: *Zef Grishaj preparing for the day's work, 5:30 a.m., Lepushe.*

Pjerin Sheldija re-working his painting of the raising of the national flag, Shkoder.

I AM PJERIN SHELDIJA; I am fifty seven years old. I was born and I live in Shkoder. I have worked since I was very young; I am a pensioner now. In 1961 I finished the high school for the arts in Tirane but I could not continue school because conditions in my family were very difficult. I began work as a teacher of drawing. I was lucky to work in the town, and I have worked very hard to maintain my position by working also with artistic groups organized outside of the school schedule. Many of my ex-students have become my colleagues.

Historical subjects attract me strongly because it is my nature. In the communist period we were obliged to work on the themes that they asked us to work on, for example, themes of national liberation or themes that had to do with the construction of socialism in Albania. In order to escape from contemporary themes, I concentrated on the historical theme of the War of National Liberation.

In those days most artists worked as teachers in the schools. The only privilege that art teachers had was reduced time in the classroom. Only a few were professionals; their salary was better. The others were paid the same as all teachers. They always gave us the colors for painting, without payment, but we had to repay them after the paintings were sold. For such exhibitions there was a commission that decided the value of each painting. They always placed a very low value on my work.

Now there is so much confusion, everyone pursues his own direction and no one is clear about which trend to follow. They all want to work like the great painters of the world, but they remain only bad imitators. There is not much chance to do modern art properly here. Artists don't know the philosophy of modern art, they haven't had many chances to go abroad to study it closely. They have escaped from the limitations of the past to a kind of unrestrained freedom and they don't know where they are going. It is a time of transition. In the past, we couldn't go beyond the limitations that were imposed upon us – they were so strict that I was forced to distort reality even in my works on historical subjects. For example, I was working on a painting on the raising of the national flag in Shkoder for an Independence commemoration. In 1912 Shkodra was occupied by Montenegro; the flag was raised again at the Castle of Rozafa on March 19, 1914. The main speaker that day was Father Vincent Prenushi. But he was an "ex-person" and I was not allowed to paint him. All the clergyman were considered bad by the regime. I painted him as a civilian, an intellectual. Now [see photograph opposite] I am returning to real history and I am putting the robes of the priest on this man.

Here is another painting, entitled "Gurakuqi Speaking." Gurakuqi is the most democratic figure in Albanian history, up to the present. The purest figure, spiritually; the most righteous one. This is a moment during his debates in the Parliament, when King Zog was still Prime Minister and the Minister of the Interior. It was the time when the opposition was fighting against the Party of Legality, which was in power. At this particular moment, side by side with Gurakuqi were Fan Noli and his adherents. The speeches of Gurakuqi and Noli were very good speeches, and they attacked the policy of the Zogu government. At that time Zogu went so far as to say: "Go on talking, because we have the majority and it is we who will decide things." A year later, in the Revolution of 1924, Noli became the head of the government. I wanted to show here the convincing force of Gurakuqi's words. Though Zogu later proclaimed himself king, the people didn't love him, except for his supporters who were mainly from the region he came from. On March 5, 1925, Gurakuqi was killed in Bari, Italy. It was a cousin of his, paid by Zog, who killed him.

One of the other figures who fought against Zogu was Bajram Curri. This painting is a little smaller, but I have painted him with love, this is one of my best paintings. Curri and his men had decided to cross the Valbona River on a log. He never parted from his rifle. On March 25, 1925,

the same month that Gurakuqi was killed, Zog's men found out through some spies where Bajram Curri was. They surrounded him in a cave and started fighting, and Bajram Curri fought till his last moment with his rifle in his hand. Bajram Curri was the Minister of the Defense in the 1924 Noli Government, while Gurakuqi was the Minister of Finance. When Curri was killed he was found with so little money in his pocket that it was barely enough for his daily expenses.

The woman in this painting was one of the first teachers in Shkoder in the time of the Turkish occupation. At that time, schools were organized in houses; reading, writing, and arithmetic were taught. The shawl on this woman's head was a kind of headdress used by women who decided not to be married but to stay at home. They were not nuns.

Here is a painting of another hero, a popular leader of our city of Shkoder. His name is Dasho Shkreli; he was the leader of a popular uprising against the Turkish invaders. I have tried to represent here all three costumes of the city, which represent the alliance between different religions. When it came to fighting against invaders, people didn't count religious differences – they considered themselves as brothers.

This is Marin Barleti. He was the first to write the history of Skanderbeg, and also of the Siege of Shkoder. He was present at that siege. Then, after most of the Albanians left and went to Venice, he left too, and he wrote about it there. No portrait of him has remained, but trying to use my imagination and with some guesswork, using some of the characteristics of the faces of the mountaineers of the north, I have tried to create this portrait.

This is a woman from Kelmend. She is doing house work, working with wool, and at the same time singing to her child. Of course she sings with a *lahute*, a traditional instrument. She sings heroic songs, songs that tell of deeds against the enemies and of the fight to defend the homeland. She is the Albanian mother who educates her children with the spirit of patriotism, of Albanian nationalism, from the time that they are in the cradle.

Above: *Bajram Curri crossing the Valbona River.*
Below: *Woman from Kelmend. (Paintings by Pjerin Sheldija)*

MY NAME IS LUCIA SERREQI. My husband Lini was a captain in the army. When we returned to Shkoder in 1946, he was told that his brother, a priest in Dukagjin, was in prison. My husband went to Tirane to plead for his brother because he was innocent, but he was sentenced to one hundred years in prison – for life. My husband sometimes had a job, sometimes not. After five years I was not allowed to work because he had been an officer and his brother was in prison. So I worked at home – I sewed.

When my husband needed to find another job, he called his friend Moise Ardite. Moise was Jewish. During the holidays my husband invited him to his home in Shkoder and he lived here for one week. Moise's father Zhak worked in a pharmacy and Moise worked with him. It was a rich family. Zhaku had four children, three sons and one daughter. Zhaku moved to Shkoder and opened a pharmacy, but Moise stayed in Tirane. He married the daughter of the consul of Czechoslovakia in Albania, whose name was Stella. Now their daughter is fifty three years old! In 1943, during the German occupation, Moise called the family in Shkoder and told them to hide because the Germans wanted to get them. Zhaku didn't think it was a serious problem, but Moise was afraid. Moise, his wife, and two children, hid in Tirane with a family named Korno – they hid in their home. Zhaku stayed in Shkoder and did not hide. When the Germans came to Shkoder they knocked at Zhak's door. He was not there, but they took Moise's brothers, sister, and mother and killed them on the street.

Moise stayed in Tirane. The family built a new home, a very beautiful home. When the [communist] Party of Labor came to power it was taken. Then Moise and his family came to Shkoder. They lived in a very small home and Moise worked in the pharmacy here. Stella had studied at the University of Vienna, in two faculties. Each year her Austrian friends sent bread for Passover. When democracy came, the family was allowed to go to Israel. Stella always wrote in her letters, "Write to me because I love Albania." Stella has died but Moise has not forgotten me. I received a letter from him two weeks ago. He is eighty eight years old. He asked in the letter for the health of Albania.

Lucia Serreqi at her desk, Shkoder.

MY NAME IS SIMON PEPA, Doctor of Science. I spent over ten years studying and preparing my thesis, going all over northern Albania, visiting all the villages, Dukagjin, Shllak, Vermosh, etc. It took me years to prepare it, from 1978 to 1988. During this time I was working as a teacher.

My thesis is one of the first dictionaries of the Albanian language in the terminology of a certain field. The words are connected mainly with agriculture, with different names of plants, different names of cultivated vegetables and so on and so forth. I prepared this thesis under very difficult conditions, of course. Nevertheless, nothing has been published yet. Half of it, three hundred fifty pages, is theory. The other half, three hundred fifty pages, is the dictionary itself. This is a linguistic as well as philological vocabulary. That is, all the words are connected to all their different meanings and to all the contexts in which they might be used, as well as the customs and mythology related to the words.

Through the vocabulary and the meaning of the word the economic richness of Albania becomes evident. I mean the vast variety of plants that can be cultivated here. For example, take the pear: there are almost eighteen phrases related to this fruit, indicating that people in the past cultivated eighteen varieties. But if you go in the zone of Kastrat now, you'll find almost nothing. Also there are many new words in this vocabulary, words that are not included in the *Vocabulary of the Albanian Language* of 1980, which is the largest published up to now. There is an Albanian word *parmenda*, which is a wooden plow. In the *Vocabulary* there is no phrase related to this word, while in mine there are twelve of them; there are also interesting points in connection with etymology and ethnography. For example, each peasant, before starting to work with his *parmenda*, had to clean and wash himself and dress in white, because it was considered a sacred tool. It can't be touched unless you are clean. It is very curious to note that this is a tradition more than five centuries old. In the sixteenth century, Budi, who was among the first to use the written Albanian language, mentions this tradition of dressing in white while using a *parmenda*. And there is also the idea that if your *parmenda* breaks, it means that you weren't properly cleaned before using it.

Another interesting tradition is that of blood smearing. Blood sacrifice is a custom that can be found all over the world. For example, they say that a woman was walled up alive in Rozafa Castle. Poles, Bulgarians and Czechs have the same legend: when you have to build something, you have to wall someone alive. For the *parmenda*, there is an expression called blood smearing. Before using it, the farmer used to kill a turkey and paint the *parmenda* with its blood. This act was thought to bring good luck and good production. In this vocabulary you can find some old traditions of the Albanian people. There is a widely used expression here, *besa e katundit* (the oath of the village). Once every year, the heads of each family used to gather in the center of the village, which was usually close to the church. There they swore on the gospel not to touch each other's produce during the year. Our peasants have never had guards or borders for their land. I have taken the expressions and studied how they have they been used in different regions, in Dukagjin, Shale, etc. This is a real treasure of language that we have.

I published a lot of studies in the press of that time and in magazines. *Linguistic Data on the Traditions of the Albanians* is a part of my dissertation dealing with the lexicology of the Albanian language. I am also coauthor of four textbooks at the university level. And for of all them I was paid enough money to buy a jacket.

Opposite: *Dr. Simon Pepa at the window of his study, Shkoder.*

*The Pepaj family
home, Selce.*

Traditional Life in Selce

SUDDENLY, in the middle of July, our friend Anton Fistani told us that we were to leave the next day for a three week stay in the Malesi e Madhe, the Great Mountains; Pellumb Pepaj, a policeman studying biochemistry at the University of Shkoder (by correspondence), would accompany us. Pellumb did not speak English, but no matter: we had a dictionary and a grammar book, and total immersion is after all the best way to learn a language. Our first stop would be the village of Selce, where Pellumb's family lives. None of the families with whom we would stay in Selce or elsewhere in the mountains knew us or anything about us, except that we were friends of Anton and were writing a book about Albania. Though they were very poor, they opened their homes and hearts to us, and they would not accept any payment in return.

Diary Excerpt. There are beautiful gorges and cold water springs in the Selce mountains; in some places there are waterfalls and natural swimming pools. Though the mountains are sheer, crumbly rock, such farmland as exists is good and farming is productive. Still, no one has indoor plumbing, and most people are out of work. The European Community airdropped bundles of clothing here a few years ago, and that is still what people wear today. There are no longer telephones or mail or bus service. There is still electricity, but there are frequent blackouts. Many people have television sets, but they cannot receive any signals without satellite receivers, which only a few mountain families can afford. There are no labor-saving machines of any kind; everything, agricultural and household, is done by hand. Many families are subsistence poor, and the conditions are dismaying (flies everywhere, no water nearby, no refrigeration). Everywhere, we saw women wearing black, for mourning. Infant mortality is high, and so is maternal mortality. There is only one doctor for all of the Malesi e Madhe, and only one hospital, in the town of Tamare (we were told that conditions in the hospital are very poor).

Pellumb lives with his wife Ana, their two small children, his mother Moro, his father Nikolle, and his younger brother. The father gets up before dawn to walk three hours over the mountain to his field, where he works all day, returning after dark; we saw him only in the evenings. Pellumb works in Vermosh, too far for daily commuting. Ana does most of the heavy work around the house. She goes up the hill to the spring to get water, which she carries on her back in a large wooden barrel; she also collects sticks for firewood and carries them on her back in huge bundles. She milks the goats, does the cooking (on the open hearth), and keeps the flies off the baby who is strapped into his cradle.

During the days that we were in Selce, Pellumb took us to see many beautiful places and to visit many families. In the evenings, we sat in the courtyard and talked, in our limited Albanian, with Pellumb, his father, his uncle, and other neighbors. In Albania, people regularly asked us questions that Americans hesitate to ask: how old are you? what is your salary? what is your religion? The men asked us all these things and also – *are those your original teeth*? There was much interest in my wedding ring because it is gold; oddly no one showed any interest in Stan's, which is identical to mine.

Neither Ana nor Moro ever joined us, not even for morning coffee. Indeed, Ana never looked us in the face, never spoke a word to us until we said goodby.

Moro Pepaj leading her cows.

"The mistress of the house has the right to order the women of the house to fetch water and wood, to bring bread to the workers, to wash, to dispose of the slops, to reap, to hoe, or to clean." —*The Kanun of Lek Dukagjini*

Ana Pepaj collecting water.

Above left: *Nikolle Pepaj*

Above right: *Anton Pepaj*

Above: *Moro Pepaj sifting grain.*

Left: *Ana Pepaj pulling a goat from the wall.*

87

*Ana Pepaj preparing
bread at the hearth.*

Above: *The Pepaj family.*

Left: *Pellumb Pepaj and his staff of soldiers, Vermosh.*

CHAPTER THREE

TO YOUR HEALTH!
Gezuar!

Rruga 13 Dhjetori, Shkoder.

The Return to Private Life

Street scene, Shkoder.

ONE MORNING we traveled by bicycle with some friends to visit a large extended family in a village near Shkoder. Their several homes stood close to one another, shaded by grape vines and surrounded by thriving gardens. Everyone in the family was unemployed, but they were managing to get by. One woman was laying herbs and ferns that she had just gathered out to dry; later the herbs would be sold to a middle man who would resell them to pharmaceutical companies. Her brother was preparing to lead their animals – goats, sheep, cows – to the high mountains; he would stay there with them, in a shed he would build, until the

Above: *Family of four on bicycle, Shkoder.*

Below: *Shop on Rruga 13 Dhetori, Shkoder.*

weather turned cool again. Another brother had recently returned from working, illegally, in Greece; with the money he had saved, he had built a new house. I asked him how he would describe the difference between his life before, under communism, and now. "Before," he replied, "it was as if we were all in the army. Now we have returned to private life." His answer has stayed with us; it provides a context for understanding Albania today. Individuals have returned to their private lives, and so have communities.

The visitor to Shkoder cannot miss the reconstruction that is everywhere underway. Here a young person has opened a shop in the very place where his grandfather's shop stood many years before; there a city planner pours over photographs of markets of the distant past with an eye to restoring them to prosperity. Teachers are eagerly studying the educational systems of other countries, government officials are visiting other countries to learn about other systems of local and national organization.

The historic Catholic cathedral has been reopened: no traces of its recent past as a sport hall remain. A mosque is being built in the center of town, on the spot where several mosques have stood before. Albanians look back toward an idealized, distant Albanian past, and forward to an idealized, hopefully not so distant, European future. Meanwhile, they are doing their best to cope with the present, which, they all agree – it is an article of faith – is a "time of transition."

On the surface, Shkoder is more prosperous than when we first visited in 1992. It is certainly much livelier, especially in the summer evenings when the sun goes down and it is a little cooler and people of all ages throng the streets and parks. Two years ago there was almost nothing to buy; now you can buy almost anything – if you have the money. Many city homes now have some modern appliances, and many peasants now have color TV, sewing machines (treadle type), and in some cases refrigerators. Two years ago, there were very few cars; the main modes of transportation were horse cart and bicycle (we saw, more than once, families of four riding along on a single bike). Today bicycles continue to be a major mode of transport in Shkoder, despite the rapid increase in the number of cars, but there are fewer horse carts. Everyone is busier, if not happier.

But in other respects, the material conditions of life have not improved since 1992 (and in some ways they are worse). Telephones are still rarities; there is only about one telephone per thousand people in Albania. Many homes have running water for only a few hours a day, if they have it at all. Housing in Shkoder is in extremely short supply; it is very difficult to find a house or an apartment for rent at any price. The poor find such housing as they can. Most roads are landmines of unfilled ditches and unmarked potholes, some of them dangerously large, on which bicyclists, pedestrians, drivers of horse carts and drivers of automobiles all fight for right of way. Many of the car drivers have been driving for only a very short time, as private cars were not permitted under the communists, and they drive as though they have no brakes, charging at full speed with honking horns down narrow, crowded streets. (We were assured that the town is planning to install some traffic lights.) The end of communism has brought mass unemployment, and many people have come to Shkoder from the mountains in the hope — not often fulfilled — of finding work.

Both Shkoder's signs of outward prosperity and its visible poverty reflect the very difficult problem of economic reconstruction. With teachers and doctors earning forty dollars a month, factories idle, and thousands of people out of work (and out of benefits), whence cometh the money for the newly available goods? The cafes, though popular, are nonproductive, and nothing sold in the newly opened stores is made in Albania. One answer to this riddle is not hard to find: for many if not most families, the main source of income is the money sent home by a father, son or brother

Above: *Painting traffic flow signs, Shkoder.*

Below: *Selling funnels for gasoline, Shkoder.*

Above: *Women drawing water, Shkoder.*
Below: *Public phone, Post Office, Shkoder.*

working abroad. This is a classic third-world solution: it keeps families going, and in some cases makes their lives much easier, but it does not rebuild the economy. A second pillar of the new prosperity was smuggling. Although the war in the former Yugoslavia had a negative effect on Albania's economy overall – the embargo against rump Yugoslavia disrupted normal trade patterns, and investors were wary of becoming involved in an area so close to a war zone – it also opened up vast possibilities for those willing to take some risks.

Suddenly gasoline and oil stations had sprung up everywhere along the road from Shkoder to Montenegro. At night, people told us, you could not see the water in Lake Shkoder because the lake was packed with boats plying "the trade" (the local shorthand for embargo-breaking). There were big smugglers and little ones. We spoke, off the record, with a primary school teacher who was also, as he put it, a "businessman in the time of the embargo." He cheerfully explained that he supplied transportation for the Italian–Montenegrin trade, and was also involved in cigarettes and gasoline (his car had a second tank hidden under the hood). But, he said, he probably would not be able to stay in business much longer, as powerful interests were driving out the little traders. As my grandmother would have put it, little smugglers, little businesses; big smugglers, big businesses.

Certainly the biggest problem facing the northern part of Albania is reconstruction: economic, cultural, and spiritual. In one way or another, all of the people you will meet in this chapter are concerned with this. They pose the problem in terms of discontinuities and continuities with the distant and recent past.

Reconstructing the distant past. As older people remember it now, Shkoder once was a town of thriving markets, prosperous businesses, high education, and lively arts. But the younger generation has no personal memory of that era. The new commercial society under construction now is played by different rules, if it is played by rules at all; *caveat emptor* – let the buyer beware – might be the watchword of the new Albania. But the distant past has reappeared in some forms: there has been a rapid resurrection of the prewar political parties – and prewar politics. The old issues are back, including land policies (rural and urban) and the worst legacy of the *kanun*, the blood feuds.

Breaking with the recent past. In the post-communist haste to deconstruct the state economy, agricultural and indus-

trial markets have all but collapsed. Now a generation of agronomists, out of work, retools itself as teachers and cafe owners while peasants try to feed their families with produce wrested from their tiny plots of land with hoes and scythes. Decrepit industries are up for sale, but few investors are buying them, and benefits have run out for the former workers, most of whom are still unemployed. The Parliament, in Tirane, passes laws, but many of them are not enforced. Virtually everyone, no matter what their political convictions, praised one feature of the bad old days: "the law was very strong, very hard."

The continuities are as problematical as the discontinuities.

Blending the best of the past with the best of the new. In contrast to agriculture and industry, the educational and health care systems of the communist era have not been summarily abandoned. But both systems are under pressure to evolve rapidly. Material aid is essential: both schools and hospitals are threadbare. Techniques must also be updated. The educational system was and is effective in teaching large amounts of material, but teaching students to think for themselves requires new curricula, new pedagogy. Medical care was and is free, and doctors and nurses were and

Tilling fields,
Hot i Ri.

Denisa Kolombi, teacher of eighth grade Albanian literature class, Shkoder.

are well trained, but modern medical technology requires increasing specialization. ("Imagine," a surgeon told us, "we still use ether here.")

Blending the worst of the past with the worst of the new. Old tensions – north vs. south, Christian vs. Muslim – have not abated much, if at all. Nor have issues such as corruption, inhumane prisons, political control of the courts, political vendetta, and restrictions on the media and on speech, though people are understandably reluctant to speak about them.

And then there are new issues, new problems. One of the most difficult is the task of reintegrating into society the people who had been persecuted by the communists for political offenses. Thousands of people were sentenced to long years in prison or forced to live and work at hard labor in remote mountain villages. In the spirit of the *kanun*, whole families were severely punished for the behavior of a single member.

Now these people have been released from prison and the remote villages, but where shall they live, and how shall they be compensated? The government has instituted preferential policies to help them with housing and other necessities. But many people – not only the formerly persecuted – believe that not enough has been done in this direction, while others believe it has already gone too far. There is controversy over the way that existing policies are applied in practice. There is also controversy over the political demands that some of the former prisoners are making.

And so, Albania is returning to private life, with all its problems and possibilities.

Opposite: *Restoring family graves, Shkoder.*

Above: *Purchasing new couch, Shkoder.*

Right: *Shkoder street market.*

Shkoder street market.

Vessel Berisha repairing
his Chinese tanker truck,
Shkoder.

Faces and Voices
the emerging present
Part I

MY NAME IS ZEF SHKRELI. I come from a family that dealt with commerce, small business. I didn't have the opportunity to finish the university, but I did finish the Jesuit school. During the communist regime I was in jail for eleven years for my political convictions; we were totally opposed to the ideas of this regime. All the building projects and all the great achievements of the communist regime were done by our hands, by people in jail. I was sentenced to twenty three years in prison, but I worked hard, and I was released after eleven years. When I came out in 1964 I was around forty. Then I married Tatjana – I could say she was the gift of communism. After that, I worked for five years at heavy labor, digging ditches, working on street repairs under the sun, etc. Suffering made us into monsters. My skill is the trade, small business, but I was obliged to do every other kind of job to survive. Now we have no aid from the state, from the government, and we are obliged to work for others. I have a small office as a representative of business, it is on Rruga 13 Dhetori, and I try to do my best.

Shkoder's society is continually changing, in the good and bad sense of the word. A new nucleus of society, without tradition, is being created. Shkoder is a city with traditions centuries old. But, unfortunately the communists tried to destroy them. Some traditions survived, but now they are at risk once again. The healthy, representative, body of society of Shkoder is not in power at the top. They are trying, but some other elements are profiting on the shoulders of honest people. Well-educated people are difficult to find in Shkoder. Unfortunately, even the people who come from abroad don't understand us, don't help the right people. Shkoder suffers for many things, but most of all for wise people.

There are no specialists in small business, in trade. There are speculators who buy materials here and sell there, for profit. We call these people *matrapas* – it is a Turkish word that means a kind of gambler in business. As I understand it, if we create business societies with good reputations, serious people, we can avoid these speculators and deal properly with trade, with commerce, with relationships in business, and so on. But the laws are not on the side of honest people; at the moment, they are on the side of speculators.

Interior of Fabrika e Tekstileve, Shkoder.

*Zef Shkreli in his
office, Shkoder.*

MY NAME IS FAIK HOXHA. I was born in 1930, in Shkoder. After I finished elementary school, I went to study at Medreseja School of Tirane. First we were taught the laws of the Islamic religion and the Arabic language, and then everything needed to become religious missionaries. After graduating from the school I started working in the Medreseja School in Tirane. Now I am the Grand Mufti of Shkoder. I am responsible for all the [Muslim] religious activities of the District of Shkoder. This includes the religious education of the people and also supervising the way my subordinates carry out their duties in the city and in the villages. There is a lack of cadres because, as you might know, during the fifty years of the communist regime no religious missionaries were trained. I am obliged to perform a lot of other duties in the mosque, to teach in the Medreseja, and to direct some training courses.

The children and the young people are showing a growing interest in religion. As for the older people, they have been always interested in religion. The ages that we have problems with are those between thirty and fifty. They have been educated with atheistic ideas.

One thing that we have been very impressed with in Albania is the religious tolerance and the good relations among religions. How did this come about?

It is the tradition of our people. Our parents, by tradition, maintained good relations between Muslims and Catholics. We inherited it and we are trying every day to strengthen this tradition. We are all Albanians and sons of God and our unity will help us in our prayers and in better performing our religious duties. It will help us also to be one independent nation. The leaders of the two religions suffered under the dictatorship. We have both been in prison, and this has brought us closer to one another. It has also had a great impact on the believers.

After the democratic changes, people were free to believe and exercise their religion. People of both religions in Shkoder showed their love for religion and God; this was manifested by the fact that everyone, adults and children, assisted in the inaugurations of the first church and the first mosque here. Through hard work and with the help of God we hope to be able to reconstruct the good tradition of faith that was completely destroyed by the Enver Hoxha dictatorship. The city of Shkoder was the first to undergo changes after the democratic movement started.

The place where the new Mosque will be constructed is the very place where it had been two hundred years ago. It was destroyed by the earthquake of 1905. It was reconstructed after that and then it was destroyed again by the dictatorship in 1967. Now we are reconstructing it for the third time. It will have one big dome, nine cupolas and two minarets. There will be a park of about eight hundred square meters, and a wonderful fountain in front of it. The capacity of the mosque will be about one thousand five hundred people. It is a Turkish project but there will be Albanian advisors as well.

Is there anything else that you'd like to tell us, that you'd like us to understand?

I appreciate the help that your country has given to us since the time of President Wilson and also today, when President Clinton is in office. I have to add that I have heard that President Clinton sympathizes with the Albanian cause and especially with Kosove and he will help us with that.

Opposite: *Faik Hoxha in his office at the Islamic Center of Shkoder.*

MY NAME IS DIELL NDOCAJ. I'm sixty years old. I have been married for forty years. We have a lot now. In the past we used to be fed only with Leshnica flour and some cheese and could hardly stand straight on our feet. While now, those who work have a chance to earn money and to have everything and be happy. Those who don't work find it very hard to survive. The land is not so good here. Even if you work hard, you are not able to produce anything. We have suffered a lot in the past. We didn't have enough bread to eat. We had no clothes, we went barefoot, while now we have a lot of clothes. I don't know what more to say. God bless you.

We see that your sons have begun to build a new house but it is unfinished. Have you had difficulties with that?

We have neither money nor building materials. The only way left is to sell the cow. But we can't do that, because it is the cow that keeps us alive. Nevertheless, it is much better now. No more Enver Hoxha's time. We suffered a lot from him. He was not religious. We don't want him any more.

Some *raki* or coffee?

Diell Ndocaj, Budaç.

Ahmet Osja in his apartment, Shkoder.

MY NAME IS AHMET OSJA, I am fifty five years old. Before I retired I was the director of the Maize and Rice Research Institute. And for a few months, during the transition, I was the Minister of Agriculture.

The ancient Greeks favored collaboration, the hybridization of thought. If two men exchange apples, they have gained nothing because they still each have an apple. But if they exchange thoughts, they each have two thoughts. We benefit when we discuss, when we collaborate with people who come from abroad.

Geographically this is a small area, but the resources are very good. Albania has two seas, the Adriatic and the Ionian, and near the seashore we have mountains two thousand meters high and more. In the mountain areas you have a continental climate. In the valley and at the sea shores the climate is Mediterranean, and this climate changes several times in a vertical manner. Ours is a hybrid climate, a combination that is good for the development and cultivation of vegetables and herbs and plants. Around three thousand two hundred species of plants grow in Albania; many are endemic, they exist only here. Even the settlements of prehistoric people here are built in a vertical way. In Albania you can find eleven amphitheaters that belonged to ancient times, two thousand years ago, Illyrian and others. Olympic games were held in these amphitheaters, with ninety thousand spectators.

Here the four seasons of the year are very drastic, very characteristic, and our peasants use and take advantage of each part of the season. Our underground resources are also very rich. In this small country you can find maybe all the elements of the Periodic Table. Some very important minerals are here in abundance: bichromium, copper. We have also petroleum and many sources of thermal waters. Another of the riches of our country is its river valleys; Albania has almost one hundred sixty rivers, nine of them very large. One of the major ones is the River Buna. Twenty million cubic meters of water flow into the sea. There are many days with full sun, around three hundred days a year and about one thousand three hundred millimeters of rain in a year. This is valuable for forests. Thirty six percent of our territory is covered by forests. The village of Vermosh alone has an inventory of one million cubic meters of wood.

It is known that the ancient Illyrians dealt with agriculture. Archeological research indicates that in that early ancient time, different herbs and vegetables were cultivated, all kinds of cereals for bread. And later plants, potato, tomato, were cultivated successfully under wonderful conditions. In the last thirty years twenty thousand acres of tobacco were cultivated, with a good yield of one ton per acre. Fifteen thousand acres of high quality cotton were cultivated in Albania; also cereals and maize.

During these last three years, the transition period, people have been involved in the economy for personal interest. They desert production – they sell themselves to earn money abroad, to find a job. And it is money they want – to provide their families with electronic devices, other devices. I hope that very soon we will come back once again to develop the richness we have in our country. First of all we need qualified people. Next it is necessary to have production acceptable to the foreign trade. And third, we should again value education. In these last years many people have abandoned their schools.

What would be the best way to organize agriculture now?

National property is not in opposition to personal property; it is necessary. And the people who have parcels of private property should declare to the government, to the state, what goals they have in mind for them. Albania lacks this. Second, just because you live in a village, it does not mean that you should deal with agriculture. Sixty five percent of the people deal with agriculture today, for personal production. It introduces a narrow mentality, a backward mentality – to live for one's self. Another thing is that Albanians are not prepared to deal with money; they don't think of putting money in the bank. Everybody takes the cash. But the maternity of money is not in the house, but in the bank.

The next important item is cooperation. We have the notion that collaboration is not mutually desirable, that somebody is going to take advantage of us or make a profit. For this reason we don't know where to invest. Another item is that we have around four hundred kilometers of seashore, but we don't take advantage of the nature we have. Half of the food is in the sea and we get nothing from it. The ports are not suitable. We know from history that one of the major elements of Roman imperialism was the Via Egnatia – twenty two hundred years ago they built roads to the extreme Orient, and this road passed through Durres. Today we have a small road, five or six meters wide, no more, very narrow.

Agriculture is very important for us. But our diet is not well balanced to satisfy our physiological requirements; we don't have a good concept of nutrition. It is important – it is necessary – to have a strategy for agriculture. The government should have an agricultural policy to support the production of the country and to support also specialization in this field. I teach a course now in which some of the students are agronomists, veterinarians, and zoologists. They are jobless now, because of the privatization. They are obliged to get another diploma to become teachers. You can imagine what it is like for a person with a high education, a good agronomist, forty or fifty years old. Many of them are women. If we continue in that way, we are going to lose a generation of specialists. For this reason I propose a policy with continuity – to conserve the specialists of agriculture. It is a duty which goes beyond the limits of the profession, it is a national duty.

*Gjovalin Luli, Inspector
of Education for the
District of Shkoder.*

MY NAME IS GJOVALIN LULI. I am fifty three years old. I was born and grew up in Shkoder. I graduated in mathematics from the university here.

The Luli family is an old family in this town; it came originally from the mountains of Shkoder. This house was built about sixty years ago. It is the fourth house built by our ancestors. The tradition of the Luli family was the silversmith trade. We used to make rings, earrings, medallions of silver and other metals, for the brides of Shkoder, Zadrime (especially Zadrime) and Mirdite and others in the mountains. My grandfather and my father, and I too, were taught that trade, but later I studied to be a teacher. Near Lake Shkoder and the Buna Bridge there were more than two thousand shops and that is where we had ours too. I worked with my father in his shop. Those shops were something special and wonderful. The area was divided into different zones – one for the silversmith trade, others for butchers, grocers, and there was a big store for different materials. The silversmith zone was called *kuigji*. But unfortunately they are completely destroyed now. They'd serve as monuments of culture if they were still there.

Now we have many problems with our economy, but we hope to do something in the future, because in Shkoder there are many handcrafters who are famous not only here in Albania, but throughout the Balkans as well. The City Council and the people are planning to revive the tradition of handcrafting silver, wood, etc. At the same time we want to revive the connections we have had in the past with our neighbors and other Balkan countries. Fortunately, this trade center was located in the place where the Buna River meets Lake Shkoder and the sea, something that makes possible connections and relations with other countries and places.

What work do you do?

I started working, first in Sarande, as a teacher of mathematics. I work now at the Board of Education of the District of Shkoder where I deal with problems of educational planning. There are many important problems of education in our school system and the first of them all is the consolidation of the system and putting it on a contemporary base. We have a Ministry of Education and Board of Education in each District that are subordinated to the Ministry of Education. All the schools of the District are dependent on the Board of Education of the District as far as problems of education and teaching are concerned, while when it comes to the administrative and financial sides of their function, they are dependent on the respective communes or City Councils.

I am a member of the City Council. We take care of the different problems our city has, for example the problems of education, of economy, of culture, of welfare, etc. But we are not able to do much about unemployment. They are trying to create jobs for people, encouraging them to work with the traditional handicrafts of Shkoder. That's why we are trying to establish relations with other cities in different parts of Europe. We try to attract investors and interest foreign companies in opening their business here, but that is difficult.

Is there anything else you'd like to say about your life, your family, or about Albania?

I would like very much to say something. One year ago some American professors came to our house through the Rector of the University of Shkoder, who is a childhood friend of mine. He wanted to bring these professors here because he was sure that the place was decent and safe for them. To be honest, at the beginning my family felt somewhat uncomfortable, and I, too, felt the same way. I had never had the chance to speak to such people and I wasn't able to imagine how would I be able to keep them in my house, how was I supposed to behave with them. But I understood very soon that we were lucky to have them here. It is unbelievable for me to see my children talk to you and discuss different issues with you. I graduated high school with excellent results – a gold medal. I had many dreams at that time, I dreamed of studying abroad. But there were no chances for me then. Now I hope my children would be lucky enough to do that.

MY NAME IS FILE PELLUMBAJ. I live in Vermosh with my small grandson. I was born in Broje. I moved here when I married.

The wood in this house is very beautiful. Is that customary in this region?

The houses built at the same time as this are like it, decorated. But not so with the new houses. They are different. This house was built fifty years ago. Kol Preka did the decoration, but he has died. In the past this house was the most beautiful of all. Now there are other houses that are more beautiful, as they are new. At the time I came here it was only a cottage; in the beginning we were very poor. Then things started to improve. We built the house. Then my brother-in-law died and a lot of other hardship followed. My husband died a year ago, my daughter-in-law two years ago. My son has been abroad for one year. He is always in danger there because he is working illegally. But he's doing well now. He's working on an island. I think he gathers fruits, but I don't know, as I do not communicate with him directly. But he works in agriculture. He is very sad, he doesn't like to come here. He has to come to his son, but not to live here forever. His wife is dead, and so . . .

Opposite: *File Pellumbaj at her dry sink, Vermosh.*

Ndrece Dedaj,
Prenda Kusia, and
Zef Kusia in front of
their tunnel home,
near Shkoder.

MY NAME IS NDRECE DEDAJ. I was born in 1943. Thanks very much for coming here to see how the Albanian people are living, to see how we work and live. I am speaking for myself, for my own. I am from Tropoja, a northern area. I have been here in this area two and a half years. Because of the difficulties of my life there, I had no place to live, so I came here with my wife and five children. And here I am also facing difficulties. It is not so easy to change at once from one system to another. I have no house, I am living in a tunnel. You can imagine how difficult that has been. We are hoping for the future. Maybe the future will be better.

Prenda Kusia in the kitchen area of her tunnel home, near Shkoder.

MY NAME IS PRENDA KUSIA. My father was poor, but we had our house. Now I have ended up in a tunnel. I have only twenty kilos for preparing bread, no more. Life is extremely difficult. I am not afraid to say these things to you because even during the communist period I said what I thought. I think that nobody wants to help us in such circumstances. Now we are in the worst situation to raise our children. We have no money, we have no jobs.

MY NAME IS TATJANA SHKRELI. I finished high school. For the past three months I have been the director of a textile enterprise organized by Albanians and Italians. *What happened in between?*

After finishing high school, the gymnasium, I was denied permission to go to the university; the reason was my father. He was secretary of the party of King Zog. When I was twenty months old, he tried to escape to go abroad, to save his life. Any right to higher education was denied to me. I was obliged to work at one of the heaviest jobs; I worked there for six months. Then I was sent off to an isolated life in a camp, a compulsory camp, totally isolated, like in an island gulag. It was in the village of Llushnje, in the swamp of Karavaste. I was there for two years. We didn't get permission to come back to our city where we used to live. They suggested that we go somewhere else. We went to Elbasan. There I started to work with sewing machines, to repair dresses, to secure the minimum food for every day. My mother found a job in Elbasan. At that time I was engaged to Zef.

I was married in Shkoder. Here, at the beginning, I started working with sewing machines. Then I worked in a factory repairing objects made of gypsum. Later I found a job in handicrafts, making chairs, baskets. Then once again, I came back home, working and giving lectures on using sewing machines to prepare dresses for women. For six months I studied to be the director of this enterprise and to be responsible for it.

This is a small manufacturer that produces dresses. Or sometimes semi-finished products come from abroad and we prepare them here. After that the clothes go back to Italy. There they are finished, they are dyed, and then they are sold in different places in the world. This manufacturer works even for Valentina. Valentina is a famous name.

We have forty four workers at the moment, including those working at home. The idea is to to enlarge the factory in the future and to have a large number of people working there. It has a good future.

I am responsible for the work inside the factory, and also for the people working outside the factory, the people who work in their homes. I think that to be successful in the manufacturing business it is necessary to take care, to be concerned that everything will be ready. I am responsible for all these tiny things that are connected with the entire strategy of the work. I am also responsible for the relations with the owner in Italy, who is a woman. It is necessary to translate documents into Italian and Albanian and everything that is related to her goes through me in Albania.

Many American and other European clothing manufacturers have the work done in another country, usually a third world country at very low wages, and then it is sent back for finishing in the United States and sold as a United States product. Is that the situation here?

This is the principle problem. Geographically, we are very close to Italy and other countries of Europe. So they send the product here, or the semi-product, for one day, or for forty eight hours. And tomorrow they get the finished product. We know everything about this problem. We understand, but we have no other choice. In these conditions we can consider it a good fate for us, even to be paid very poorly. Especially the handicapped. There are hundreds of people waiting behind the doors to try to get these jobs.

Opposite: *Tatjana Shkreli examining a sweater at the Fabrika Tekstileve, Shkoder.*

MY NAME IS BERNARD PJETER LULI. I am fifty one. I graduated from the University for Physical Education. First I was appointed as a teacher at the high school in Koplik, where I worked for five years. Then I was transferred to a high school near the Mes Bridge, about six kilometers from Shkodra. I worked there for eighteen years. I used to ride a bicycle to work everyday. There were buses available too, but I thought it would be better for my health to ride a bicycle. I have been teaching physical education in the Foreign Language High School for the past six years.

What is the physical education program in the school where you teach?

The program is compulsory, two classes of physical education a week, or approximately seventy two classes every school year. The program includes athletics (the main discipline, thirty percent), basketball, volleyball, handball and some other sports in which students can participate if they like, for example aerobics, table tennis and soccer. Soccer, though it is very popular in our country, is not included in the compulsory program. There are six to eight classes in the program for swimming, but this is only for schools that are near lakes, seas or rivers, while in the mountains skiing is being taught instead, as well as traditional games. There haven't been any fundamental changes in the school programs since the communist era; they are almost the same. Now we are thinking of reconstructing them, adjusting them to the demands of the young people. Girls are interested in fitness, while boys are more interested in sports like karate.

What was the professional sports program in the communist era?

During the communist era sport was centralized, government owned. There were no private clubs. We didn't have professional sports, only amateurs. Athletes used to work at different jobs and practice sports at the same time. Now soccer is a professional sport. It is sponsored by the government, because the clubs can afford only part of their expenses. As for other sports, the government doesn't have enough funds to support them. The government is interested in having private clubs that can afford to pay their own expenses.

What do people do here for physical exercise outside school?

We don't have massive amateur activities. We couldn't have it in the past, as we had no free time. We spent it in government organized activities. People didn't have any desire for any kind of physical exercise because they were exhausted from their daily work. Now young people love to exercise, they love sports such as karate, aerobics, etc. And some physical education instructors work in their free time, in the evenings, with people who are interested. The people most interested are those who have been abroad, for example to Greece or Italy. But we need more equipment, such as balls, sportswear, facilities, and they cost a lot. Imagine, we don't even have swimming pools here. There was one in a factory; it was used only by professional athletes, they used to train there. It was used only when the factory was working. Now that it is not working, there is no warm water.

*Bernard Luli in his
vegetable garden, Shkoder.*

Dr. Anton Fistani in his Human Paleontology Laboratory.

MY NAME IS ANTON FISTANI, I was born in Shkoder in 1944. I finished high school in Shkoder and the university in Tirane. Next I became a Doctor of Science, in molecular biochemistry. I worked on proteins of different plants and other living organisms. I had a very good background in comparative anatomy, zoology, botany, paleontology, and even in geology. I have devoted myself to the paleontology of human evolution at the University of Shkoder.

Paleontology without fossils makes no sense. First it was necessary to discover the fossils. In 1977, when I began in this field, the general idea in Albania was that this country has no fossils. I was surprised at this. In fact, during the 1980's I discovered some sites which produced fossil material, rare material. These sites are southeast of Shkoder, in Gajtan, Baran, and in other sites in Rragam. There are others in the south of Albania and in other areas. In the caves of Gajtan, the discoveries belong to Middle Pleistocene period – we have discovered a large fauna which specify this time. We have discovered macacus, rhinoceros, bison, and many species which belong roughly to a period half a million years ago. It is difficult to speak about the cultural level at that time, but in a way this means that *homo erectus* existed in Albania, visited Albania. He made stone tools, which he left in the caves. Apparently we have no remains of this species of human being from this period of the evolution of mankind. But for the later periods, we have a lot of caves, a lot of rock shelters, a lot of sites which have not been studied yet; Albania was a *tabula rasa* in that sense, but now it is changing.

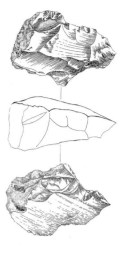

Hand-axes discovered in the lowermost levels of Gajtan I site (ca. 600,00 BCE).

In Gajtan, between 1981 and 1994, I also discovered some material from the Upper Paleolithic period. The stone tools are more polished, prepared with a higher level of skill. And there I discovered the carved stone which I presented at Smith College and at the Congress of Zaragoza. I think it must be around thirty thousand years old – from the time when the transition from Neanderthal to *homo sapiens* was occurring, in the last glacial period. The stone is a small piece of material, fifteen centimeters long, two flat areas which are incised with horizontal lines. When I discovered it I thought at first that it was made by nature, an accident. But when I saw that the material is not very hard, but is soft, and the hardness of the stone is similar to that of chalk, I was convinced that is was made by a human being. When I saw the next layer of the stone, after I washed it in water, there were the same lines – seven lines and eight lines. Such things have been discovered in other countries, which made me sure that we were dealing with an act of a human being. It is very interesting that a man who flaked stone, prepared stone tools, lived in caves, had rituals, hunted wild animals, would have such developed mathematical thinking. It testifies that prehistoric civilizations in Albania had reached such a level.

The prehistory of the Stone Age was totally unknown in Albania. Now a lot of material is being published and a large cooperative research program is in progress with people in different countries.

This room was a kind of biochemistry laboratory in the beginning, empty, there was nothing scientific inside. Slowly, slowly, day by day, we gathered different materials. Now there are hundreds of specimens of different rare species. Much of it still isn't published because I haven't had time. I had to be a photographer, an illustrator, a digger, and a scientist at the same time. And I also had to give lectures in chemistry in order to live – otherwise I was not paid.

To understand the future it is necessary to understand the past, especially for Albania. If we go back in time we see that Albania has a special history. It was under Turkish occupation for five centuries and many of the worst "misteachings" that still remain in this country and in this people come from that time. I don't like to blame our problems on this past history because we must do things for ourselves in the future. But to improve here is not so easy. And to do research, especially, is not so easy. This laboratory is known in the world now. It is a good starting place for research in paleontology in Albania. We have a rich collection of fossil material, and also vestiges of prehistoric culture, different tools, different stones, the carved stone. And now I have a specialized library, my personal library, that I can lend to anybody who would like to devote himself to this subject.

MY NAME IS MARIJE SHELDIJA. I was born in Shkoder in 1947. I am married; my husband Pjerin and I have three boys, nineteen, sixteen, and thirteen. The eldest one is in a scientific school in Italy. I am an English teacher and the head of the school for foreign languages here in Shkoder. We have about six hundred students; they come from the northern part of Albania. There are fifty teachers in my school – they are good teachers. We teach English, German, French, and Italian.

There is a competition to enter the school; we take students according to our plan. For example, this year we are going to take about sixty students in English, thirty in French, thirty in Italian, and fifteen in German. In the first year, they begin the language of their first choice, and then in the second year they begin to study another language as well.

This school is a pedagogical school too; it began as a language school ten years ago. I began there only two years ago. I had been teaching in an elementary school; I have been teaching English for twenty seven years, beginning when I was twenty years old and had finished the university. But I have not practiced the language for twenty five years. I have read English and I am not afraid to teach English. But, when I speak English I am a little afraid and confused because I have not practiced the language for so long. I feel that I make mistakes a lot of times. But the important thing is that I understand I make mistakes. I began my work in this school as a vice director. But now this year I have become the director. I don't know whether it is good or bad that I have accepted it, but I will do my best to do the job properly.

What it is like for you and your husband today as parents of teenage boys?

For parents in America and for us, it is a difficult period because teenagers think they know everything but in fact they know nothing. As I have said to them, it is the age of flying. At first I tried to work with them but I had to interrupt that because I had to work in the afternoon. I didn't understand that I was making a great mistake. I feel it now, but it is a little late. But I had to work because my husband couldn't. During that time my husband worked with them too, but I think it's the mother that the children need more than the father. Perhaps I am wrong. But they didn't give me any great problems. I don't want to say that I am traditional or fanatic, that there are some things that I can't accept. For example, we have educated them to be polite and to be sincere. But, I see that sometimes they act as they like to act. And when I criticize them, they say, "Oh mother, you are old now, you don't understand us, our problems." We want them to come home at nine o'clock when it is summer and to tell us where they want to go. This is a problem that I have discussed with my children and sometimes they say, "We don't know ourselves where we are going, I say to you I am going out, I am leaving, but I don't know where I am going because you know that I have no place to go." But I am always afraid when they are out. We never think of good things, we always think of bad things. But, to tell the truth, their life is sad.

Opposite: *Marije Sheldija in prayer, the Cathedral of Shkoder.*

Gjon Kola with script, Shkoder.

MY NAME IS GJON KOLA. I was born in 1946, in Tirane, and studied at the Institute of the Arts there. Now I work as an actor in the Migjeni Theater in Shkoder.

I never wanted to be an actor. It happened quite by accident. My parents had suffered in the mountains, where you have hiked, because they were a persecuted family. I had always dreamt of becoming a construction engineer, or an architect, but at that time we weren't able to fulfill our dreams. The people who were classified as having bad *biografi* were doomed to the less preferable branches of study, and I was offered mining engineering. But my parents were ready to sacrifice a lot for me, so they agreed to my plan to fail the first class, so that I would have a chance to change my field of study, and in that way hope for a life different from theirs among the mountains, with so many difficulties that you, yourselves, have been able to see. During my studies I had to show that I was a very bad student, which would allow me to automatically change my specialization. I had a lot of free time, so I was able to attend the performances of the National Theater frequently. I hadn't been there more than nine or ten times when people working in the Institute of Arts, where I used to look for tickets, some of them directors, invited me to become an actor. It was a decision made by People's Artist Pjeter Gjoka and by the persecuted director Michael Luarasi, who has studied in Hungary and is working there now, with Hungarian TV. They hoped that they would make a great actor out of me. They coached me to take part in the competition for entering the school, because up to that time I knew nothing about that profession. Then I started working in the theater.

I am not sure how good I have been. I have played in several movies; I have even played the main character in one or two of them. For example, I played in the TV-film *Flaka e Maleve* ("The Blaze of the Mountains"). It was a serial. There were discussions at the Fifth Albanian Film Festival of giving me a special award for that role. And also I have played different roles in the theater. This has been characteristic of me: as I have had no particular support, no one to favor me, I have had the chance of having a wide range of roles. My favorite role is the one you have seen, Archibald in the tragicomedy of Hugo Bette, an Italian author.

Are there roles that you'd have loved to perform that you didn't have the opportunity to play?

I dare not say it – Don Quixote. And Hamlet is one of my dreams. The book that I keep under my pillow is a book of comments about *Hamlet*. But I am not a utopian. I don't dare to hope.

What is the state of theater and arts in general in Albania today, especially in Shkodra?

The state of the theater is very difficult. The authors are not reflecting the changes, the new life, the current issues and problems of the society, the present developments in their dramas. Another specific problem is that the audience is, not in the bad sense but in the good sense of the word, waiting for Godot, waiting for new trends, for new solutions in art. There are also economic problems. We don't have sponsors; we don't have funds.

Are you satisfied with your work?

No, I'm not satisfied. We have had a real inquisition here. We have interpreted roles which made us blush on the stage, and we blush when we remember them now. I am speaking in the name of all my colleagues who have interpreted roles that went against our desires, false roles. Unfortunately, through them we have supported a kind of dictatorial ideology. But, though I am not hap-py to admit it, I have remained like a child eager for work. I am getting old, but my dream remains the same.

We'd like to understand this a little better because, for example in Russia, under communism, the theater was still excellent. Why was it different here?

In Albania the isolation was more terrible than anywhere in the world. Russia has other traditions, stronger than ours. Five centuries of Ottoman occupation, fifty years of dictatorship and then, in order to create the new ideology, all the culture of the past was forbidden. So far did this go, that when it came to approve the official language, they didn't approve the language used by two-thirds of the population, but they forced the one used by the town the dictator was born in. Professor Arshi Pipa has declared that the struggle for the official language of the dictator was a struggle against the North, Gegeria, against the Christian-Catholic literature, against Fishta, Budi, Bogdani, Harapi. Enver Hoxha buried them all. He went so far as to have the printing presses constructed without certain marks used in the Gheg dialect.

During the fifty year period of communism, starting from the capital, the level of the arts declined gradually. They deprived people of the best pieces of music of the other countries. They also encouraged the cultivation of a kind of oriental music, the music of the Gypsies. They stripped literature, drama and movie characters of their very spirit. Dualism was nowhere to be seen – the inner world of the characters was nowhere to be seen. They tried to create the Robot Man – without soul, without thought, ready to comply – a man without a head.

Now there is freedom everywhere. There are financial and technical problems, strongly related to the difficulties of the transition period. And while the cost of living has increased, let's say ten times, the salary of an artist remains very low. I am very anxious, because unfortunately time is passing by and many witnesses, people who have lived to see many things, are passing away and I don't know when we, the artists, will be able to bring them to art. Because we have been censured for fifty years, and another five hundred years conquered, what we have been able to save up to now, it would have been better to reflect in our works.

Gjon Kola in the role of Archibald in a play by Hugo Bette, Migjeni Theater, Shkoder.

Muhamet Gonjolla painting the mountains of Lepushe.

MY NAME IS MUHAMET GANJOLLA. I was born and I have lived in Shkoder. I work at the Migjeni Theater. I graduated from high school but didn't have the chance to continue my studies at the university, because of the conditions of that time. I have spent my time painting since I was a child. My grandfather and my uncle were both artists. My dream is to go ahead in this profession. I have traveled a lot, too. Nature has always been my primary subject. It is there that I find real pleasure.

In the past it used to be very difficult to get canvas and oils, but it is not now. They are a little bit expensive, but we are able to find anything we need in Tirane.

I hope you will come to Shkoder and have a chance to see my pictures. But don't expect to see miracles. I have taken part as an amateur in all the exhibitions organized in Shkoder and I plan to open an exhibition of my own now. I have over two hundred pictures. But time will show what is going to happen.

I AM FILIP GURAZIU. I come from a persecuted family of Shkoder; my father was killed by the communists.

When I was young I used to practice sports, basketball, and so, thanks to my talent I was able to go to the university to study mathematics. I began teaching in the mountains and villages, but then they wouldn't let me teach anymore because of my family background. I was a worker in an agriculture cooperative and later a bookkeeper, and it was only in these last years of democracy that I began to work again as an educator and as a principal of a high school. And now, I have been elected the Mayor of Shkoder, representing the Democratic Party.

We are following the American model, because I was there for a month to learn from the American experience. The American model is very wide and general, because different cities in America do things differently. But the main thing that I got from the U.S. is the check and balance principle, that I, as the mayor, follow in my relations with the City Council.

Mayor Filip Guraziu in his office, Shkoder.

At first my staff was thirty eight officials, while now there are sixty four. There is a City Council, of thirty one persons; one of them is Mr. Luli. There are three socialists in the council, and there are ex-communists; they have changed their appearance but they haven't changed at all. We have representatives of the Democratic Party, the Socialist Party, and the Republican Party, and the Social Democratic Party. The political life here is very quiet; we get on very well with each other and we respect one another. The council has a chief who is elected by the council members. The council is divided in groups, for the economy, for education, and for foreign affairs.

We took power at a time when everything had been destroyed. This happened in other countries of the East [Bloc], but Albania had its own peculiarities, because those who were in power destroyed the country with a devilish strategy. It may seem strange to you but the old system devised a plan to pay the workers eighty percent of their salaries just for staying home. It lasted more than a year. People stayed at home and received the salaries, and the companies remained empty, with no work to be done. The workers had nothing else to do but steal material and equipment from the government-owned companies. They considered the common property as their own and they thought that they had the right to take it, because they had been so exploited by the former government that it seemed normal and right to them to take things home. Albania was intentionally destroyed, as if it had just passed through a war. When my friends learned that I was going to become the Mayor, they advised me not to accept it, because they thought I would surely fail politically. They told me that I wouldn't have any political future after that. But it is of no great importance to me. I do not see myself as a politician in the future. What is important for me is to give as much as I can to the democracy. My salary now is one hundred eight dollars a month; when I started in this position it was sixty dollars a month. Others, some engineers, work here for forty dollars or fifty dollars a month; I consider it heroism to work here, with such a small salary and so many responsibilities. We have to confront the demands of the population every day, of a population that is hungry and homeless, jobless. It is a great sacrifice, but we do it willingly and with passion, just to pass through this difficult period that we are in now.

As everybody had been unemployed here, as the poverty here was in a stage that you cannot imagine, it was impossible and it is still impossible to tax the population. We have just started to impose some local taxes; Shkoder is somewhat advanced in this direction, because we have started to educate our citizens about the tax system. For example, we have the right to collect taxes from the peasants who come everyday to sell their goods in the town market, and we have a tax for hunting. But these are very small amounts of money, which do not create much of a financial base for us. It is impossible to plan any serious investment in the town with this. We are trying to increase the taxes and to convince the people to pay them.

The life of the town is organized through some companies that are organized by and technically dependent on the city. But their salaries, though taken from the city's budget, are approved by the central government. Briefly, we have three great city companies, the company for cleaning, the Greenleaf Company, which takes care of the parks, and a company that looks after the roads and the ditches of the town. We are improving gradually. I am happy that you are able to see the differences. Personally I am not in the least content with the situation.

Gjergj Marena in front of his gas and oil station "Maastricht," Shkoder.

M Y NAME IS GJERGJ MARENA. I am from Shkodra and I am forty six years old. I began to learn the English language some years ago in order to have contacts with the world. By knowing an important language such as English we are better able to understand what is happening around us and to explain to others our situation in Albania. I have worked in different professions. I worked first as a welder, then in a cigarette factory. I had a lot of contacts with different people during the communist period and a Dutch journalist girl helped me to escape to the Netherlands. I went there and I saw Maastricht and Rotterdam. Then I went to Germany and worked there in an Italian restaurant. I saw how the people in the West worked, how they are engaged with each other, their attitude toward work, and it was a very good experience for me.

I was in Maastricht during the period of the meeting of the twelve countries of Europe, and as the United States is created from about fifty states, I dream also of Europe to be the United States of Europe – the same. So the name of my firm is Maastricht. I have a partner, a construction engineer, and now we have built a center for selling gas and oil. We have installed three systems with a capacity of about ninety tons altogether – thirty tons each. And also we have a construction firm with about thirty workers and two technical people. And we have our truck – about thirty tons. It's a matter of days until we can begin our work there. And also we are engaged in a business for mushrooms.

We are linked with an Italian firm, Standa, and they have come here to see the possibilities for mushrooms in this zone. They have come five or six times, to Vermosh, Lepushe . . . The big difficulty is the mentality of the people here. Some of them have a lot of doubts about whether it is possible to do business with mushrooms. Others say mushrooms are worthless. We are engaged, figuratively, in such battles, because the mentalities in Albania are so different. One person here said, this price is not high enough. But how does he know this? He says this only to create problems between people. We are gathering about one hundred kilos daily.

Now we have paid for a big refrigerator in Shkoder. We have three rooms there. One is kept at minus thirty five degrees, one at minus twenty degrees. We have at our disposition a refrigerator truck – about two tons – and we put in electrical power through the night, and during the day it's about minus fifteen degrees. So we collect mushrooms, we put them in the refrigerator truck, and we send them to Shkoder. Then we put them immediately in the big refrigerated room, the one that is minus twenty degrees. They will stay there until we have about twenty tons; then we will send them to Italy. But so far we have collected only about one ton. It was only some days ago that we began. It's expensive for us to stay in the mountains three or four days with a refrigerator truck and to return to Shkoder and to come back again. We have to pay for gas and oil and for the driver. But we hope that we will succeed in this.

There are different kinds of mushrooms here, but the most important are the *baletus*. They are strong and more resistant than the others. They are very large. They grow wild; they are not cultivated here. They can be, but animals eat a lot of them. It is a danger for us. Sheep and goats, they eat a lot.

Do you employ local people to help find them?

Yes. We weigh the mushrooms on a balance scale and we pay immediately. The people are very happy when they earn money. There is an old woman who brings about twenty kilos here every day. She was here twenty minutes ago. She is very occupied with this and she is a very good worker.

Private enterprise is relatively new for Albania. Is the government able to provide any help to new businesses?

That is the main problem in Albania because the Albanian government has a large debt, about half a billion dollars, to the West. So the banking system in Albania really is half dead, half alive. About eighty percent is dead, in my opinion. When, in a country, the main key – the banking system – doesn't work, then the private firms have a lot of difficulties. If you want to take out a loan in Albania, especially in Shkoder, the interest rate is very high, about thirty percent. How can you pay that? There is another rate for the formerly persecuted people, politically persecuted. It's a good thing to give to them first. I appreciate that. But how much or in what manner this money goes directly to these people – there are a lot of problems there.

So, we are in difficult conditions. But we don't like to say that we are dead now. No, we have begun to live, really. We work now. And we know that we work at first for ourselves, then for the others, and not as before. Before, we worked for the party, for the homeland. But the homeland didn't exist, really. Now we know that the money goes directly to us and to the workers who work for us – and not to the government. In general, the laws of the system, of the juridical system, are improving day by day.

A Housewife in Shkoder

IN ALBANIA most of the marriages aren't arranged by love. I don't know how is it in the United States. This is a very old tradition. Here in Albania, if I fall in love with a boy and I want to go out with him, it is considered shameful. Maybe this has to do with our culture. Feelings are the same for everybody, in Albania, in United States, wherever, but the way you control the feelings differs. According to the Albanian tradition, Albanian culture, it is the family that decides whether someone is going to marry somebody else or not. I am generalizing, this isn't absolutely true in every case, but usually the family decides whether the prospect is a good man or a good woman and it is they who decide whether you might be married.

As for my marriage, I knew my husband but I had never thought of marrying him. But he loved me, though he never was open about that, he didn't tell me that. He told his sister about his feelings and they discussed the possibility of the marriage with my brother. My brother asked me if I would like to marry him (I am telling a very brief version of what happened). He told me that it was up to me to decide. If I was positively sure that I didn't like it, I only had to tell him, and he would have answered in his name, saying that he didn't like the marriage and he wouldn't allow it. He would have opposed the marriage in the name of the family and not get me involved in it; I wouldn't have had to say no. I didn't know how to decide. I was at crossroads. At last I decided for it, because my brother liked the idea so much. I asked him, "Are you on his side or on my side?" And he replied, "You know, he is a very serious man." And my mother, too: she used to say: "You are not good enough for him, he is better than you." So I was at a loss. Maybe I was dreaming of other things. My mother then explained to me that married life is difficult and that I had to decide then and there. And after some thinking I decided to marry him. I was working far from Shkoder at that time, in a village.

In a Village Near Shkoder

WE HAVE PEOPLE from Dukagjini here, from Shala, and also some Muslims. My daughter is six years old. We were taking a nap, and she asks: "Father, who is worse, the Catholic or the Muslim?" I answer: "The Muslim, of course." And she thinks for a moment and then asks again: "Who is worse, the Muslim or the Shala people?" I said: "The Muslim." "So the Muslim is that bad?" Even the six year old kid knows that there is a difference between Muslims and Catholics, because they are very bad people.

The majority of the people in this village are Muslims. There is only one Muslim cafe around here. Muslims do not go to the cafes of the Catholics, they only go to the cafe of the Muslim. Or, when they come to speak about someone, who is really a good guy, with a good reputation, they say: "He is good, but he is a Catholic." Or Catholics will say, "He is good, but he is a Muslim." This is the hatred between the Muslims and the Catholics. Practically, in Albania Muslims have always been in power and they have oppressed the country. At the castle of Shkoder there were a lot of wars between the Turks and the Albanians. It is a well known fact that this region hated the Ottomans. But the Turks exercised their influence through giving the best positions, the best land to those who agreed to change their religion. Even today, the Muslims here are in possession of the best land. The contradictions between the Muslims and the Catholics are, I think, more tense here in Albania than anywhere in the world.

Are you talking about belief, for example the Koran or the Bible, or about culture?

My opinion is that it is totally based on social differences. The difference here is as great as the difference between day and night. If you go to three different houses, without previously knowing which are Muslim and which are Catholic, you can tell at once, it is not necessary to talk to the people, just to enter and see. They don't have culture. Imagine, they have turned the woman into a house woman, here in the village. Women are forced to cover their faces with veils, they have no right to go to the mosque, they have no rights at all but remain within the walls of the house. While the Catholic woman goes to the church every day, or twice a week. So she has a way of being entertained.

But the kanun of Lek Dukagjini, which rules in the mountains, is followed by the Catholics, and it is very strict against women.

We, the Catholic population, have started to abandon the *kanun*. We don't read it and even sometimes we won't allow it to enter our houses. The *kanun* is read only by people who are involved in blood feuds, because it has been hard and very specific about these cases. While as for the differences between the man and the woman, it is important to say that the house is the property of the man – only his name is mentioned (this is what is taken from the *kanun*) – but as for the economics of running the house, it is equal for both, the man and the woman. According to the *kanun* of Lek Dukagjini, you are not supposed to love the women very much, but we do love our women, better than you do in your country.

There has been something very good in the village, here and in many regions: many religious holidays, such as for Saint Nicholas, are celebrated also by all the Muslims of the region although it is a Catholic holiday. And when they swear, when they have to swear so that they want to convince you that they are not lying, they say: For Saint Nicholas. There are Muslim families here that, if you trace them back for four generations, you'll find that they were Catholics.

Above: *The sherbel plant,
Selce.*

Right: *Descending mountain
carrying fifty kilo sack of
sherbel, Selce.*

The Sherbel Cycle

A man: *I work privately at home. In summer I gather medical herbs, sherbel. It is needed as a medicine. My father deals with the animals, my mother deals with the housework, with my son. There are a lot of things that we do together, especially those that have to do with the preparation of sherbel. I don't deal with other things, I have no shop, I don't deal with trade or business. Last year sherbel was sold for nine hundred leks a kilogram – it was good then. But now it has fallen down to three hundred fifty leks. There are so many things that are very difficult. Some have managed to improve their lives, with cars, with this and with that.*

A woman: *We live up there, in the mountain. We work all the day long with sherbel. There are five of us up there. I have to take care of the child and all of the housework, from bread, to water and everything else. We get very tired. What kind of life is that? We are working our souls out. What do we need this kind of life for? Especially now that I am alone. We barely survive, especially those who cannot find water close by. Can one survive without water now? What more can I say, everything is earned with so much pain. And everything just for a loaf of bread.*

SHERBEL, a variety of sage (*salvia officionalis L.*), is an important commodity in Albania. Every day in the summertime, the people of the northern villages follow steep goat trails up into the bare, rugged, stone-strewn mountains to collect the wild *sherbel*, to pluck the plants from the rocks amidst which they grow. It is hot, terribly hot, and there is no shade. Twice a day, beginning at dawn and again in the midafternoon, men and women carry huge sacks up these mountains, fill them with fifty kilos of sherbel, hoist the loads onto their shoulders, and carry them down again. (A simple system of pulleys could save much backbreaking labor, but we saw none.) Once home, they spread the *sherbel* out to dry. Later, if they are fortunate, a middle man will come to buy it for resale to western companies.

Sherbel has remarkably many uses: a 1993 article in a Czech journal (*Cesk-Farm*) on *salvia officinalis L.* explains that "The pharmacopoeial criterion of quality is the content of essential oil, which is produced in an increased amount in the plant in warm summer months. *Herba salvia* and the extracts prepared from it are used as an antiseptic agent, an antiphlogistic agent, in the inflammations of the oral cavity and gingivitis and also as a stomachic and an antihydrotic agent. Its utilization in cosmetics and the food industry is also of importance."

We followed the trail of *sherbel* from the mountains to a giant warehouse in Shkoder, where twenty thousand tons are being kept in storage. Formerly, eight hundred people – mainly women – had worked in the plant; now there are five. The black market has destroyed the state market, the director told us. We have tried to find out where *sherbel* goes when it leaves Albania – which firms buy it, and how it gets to your pharmacy or kitchen table, but no one seems to know.

Above and left:
Drying sherbel.

Opposite page:
*Pausing to rest,
carrying sherbel,
Selce.*

Sherbel press and scale,
Enterprise for Foodstuffs,
Shkoder.

Faces and Voices

the emerging present

Part II

Fadilet Hyseni (left) unloading a fifty kilo bag of sherbel, Enterprise for Foodstuffs, Shkoder.

MY NAME IS FADILET HYSENI. I am the manager of the *sherbel* processing division of this factory.

Sherbel is used as a spice for steaks. Sometimes it is imported as an herb to prepare medicines. Sometimes they take out the extract, *oleo officianalis*. Here in Albania *sherbel* has been used in popular medicine for preparing tea for people with breathing problems.

Sherbel grows mainly in the mountains here, especially in Shiroke and Tarabosh. Taraboshi's *sherbel* is well known for its quality but *sherbel* grows in other mountains as well. It is wild, not cultivated. It is collected from May 15 until June 15. Sometimes it can be found even in lower regions, but that is not of the same quality as the sherbil found in the mountains. The percentage of tyron, that is an element of the *sherbel*, is 0.58 in this region. It is one of the best in Albania. It also grows in other parts of the Balkans, as in Croatia and Montenegro. In the south of Albania there is a kind of *sherbel* that is brighter than the one you find in Shkoder, but it is not as good. It has a lower percentage of tyron.

People mostly began collecting *sherbel* thirty years ago. Before that time there was a small center and people used to collect it in small quantities, just to fulfill the domestic needs. Later, a very small company was created in Shkoder, it started twenty five years ago; before that time you couldn't speak of an industry. But the main bases for collecting the *sherbel* have always been in Durres and at the Agro-Export company in Tirane. For thirty years now the technicians of this company have bought *sherbel*. They used to process it and then sell it through Austrian or Swiss firms to the United States, but it has never been sold through us to the U.S., because the old system wouldn't allow us to.

In the past, we didn't know anything about the price. But we knew that it was very low, though enough to provide for the workers' salaries. Now the prices have changed. Two years ago we sold one hundred fifty six tons to Albdukros, an Italian-French-Albanian company, at one dollar and sixty cents per kilogram. But for the past year we have not been able to find a market for our *sherbel*. The private firms took advantage of the situation and sold their *sherbel* at a lower price than ours. Our cost of production was higher because we paid the workers more money and we also paid for their social security. Private companies did not do that. They took advantage of the unemployment and bought the *sherbel* from people at very low prices. They sold it at eighty cents per kilogram and they made a profit at a time when our cost, without profit, was one dollar and forty cents per kilogram. Most of the *sherbel* goes to the private firms because we cannot pay the collectors. Part of it is sold abroad in very suspicious ways, without paying customs. Especially in Montenegro. Making use of the embargo, they are trying to make money in every possible way they can. It is an unprecedented situation. The government-owned companies are not able to make money under these conditions. Two years ago eight hundred women worked here. Now there are only five: two people who are in charge of the products that we keep in storage, two workers and me. In the past *sherbel* was not kept in storage for a long time, because we sold it. But in the last check we have made, we found that it is still in very good condition and there are no quality problems. We have had some offers, but we didn't agree because of the price.

As we all know, the government in Albania plans to privatize the small and medium sized companies. So our *sherbel* company might be privatized in the future. But for the moment this process has frozen.

Our main problem is getting involved in business. It doesn't matter whether this sector is private or government-owned. We want put people to work again.

M Y NAME IS LUIGJ SHYTI, I am forty six. I am a biology teacher here in Theth. We teach the students about animals, plants and the anatomy of the human body. My students prefer studying the world of plants, and especially the medicinal herbs of this area, herbs that are used to cure different diseases. Our country is rich in plants. These plants can be found from the lowest plains to the highest mountains. We have a Mediterranean – continental climate and that's the reason why Thethi alone has almost one hundred twenty identified medicinal herbs. We try to teach our students about the herbs and their usage for practical purposes. These plants are collected to be sold, exported, or to prepare drugs. They are also used in popular medicine, for example they might be used for the baths. They cure stomach, ear, eye, skin, icterus (*epatitus viralus*) diseases.

We saw that the hospital in Dukagjin has very few medicines. Do they use popular medicine there?

These plants are not properly evaluated by the official doctors. Years ago they were being used, but mainly in the home, not in hospitals. They are not studied and applied scientifically. They're used for business, because they are in great demand by the foreign trade, in the foreign market. But this doesn't influence the need our patients here have for them.

Are these ancient traditional remedies or are they newly discovered?

Some are new and others are old. But most of them have been discovered and identified recently. They are *dukla*, daisies, ferns, pine, ash trees, forest artichoke, *gerokuli*, *shtara*, the nettle, orchis, gentian, *sanza*. Thethi has a very interesting plant – its name is *Bolthania baldaci*. It is not specifically useful; its value is in its rareness.

Tom Alia, driver, Vermosh center.

MY NAME IS TOM ALIA. I was born in 1951. I have been working in this profession for twenty seven years, always in the mountains and with the same type of truck. Physically it is much easier now. In the past we were guaranteed only our daily bread. Now we have no work, but if the government would have tried a little, we'd have been much better off. What has passed may never come back again. Most of all, we have our God now and we pray to Him.

Always, in the old system and now, I have worked in the forest, carrying timber, logs, branches from the mountain. That's the only thing I know how to do. When it snowed and froze, something that happens often in these parts, before starting for home, we prayed to God, "Save us. Don't let us break our necks." But we, the drivers of the old system, were very well prepared technically. We all attended driving school for one and a half years and we have had very few accidents, considering the difficulties of the road and the terrain, as well as those very, very old trucks that were used for transportation.

After you take the wood from Vermosh, where do you bring it?

I distribute it in my area, in Shkoder and Koplik. But we have very little work to do. We do not have any work guaranteed from the government. When I travel for the government, with regular documents, I earn no more than twenty five dollars for each trip. For a trip from Shkodra to Vermoshi I have to spend forty two or forty three dollars in oil and also five dollars for some lubricant oil, because it's an old truck and it needs a lot of it. So, all that remains from what I get from the government-owned company is twenty five dollars. There are only a few trips needed and the salary is very low. These trucks were made in Czechoslovakia and only the government companies still use them. Private owners of trucks cannot afford to work with them, as they use too much oil and are not economical. As I have no money to buy a new truck, I have to work with this. I'd like to have a good truck as I am an old professional now. It's hard for me to see young drivers, in modern cars, who do not deign to travel with me in my truck.

Do you still have to sacrifice, as you did in the past?

In the past, like it or not, I was forced to work, in snow and ice. While today, I work for my own interest and we are freer. It's better.

145

MY NAME IS ROZINA LULI; I am forty two years old. I graduated from the university in construction engineering in 1974; I specialized in industrial buildings and houses. I finished high school with very good results; the field of study I liked most was mathematics. But in our country they didn't allow people to choose the field they liked most. I considered myself very lucky to have been able to study engineering. Going to the university was like a dream at that time.

We were so discontented with the old regime that the only consolation we could find was in God. I can't forget the past. And for that reason maybe I am an extremist with respect to many problems. We were the poorest country and sometimes we were afraid, and it's only in God we hoped, it's only through God that we thought that salvation would come for our country. For example, when I worked as an engineer, my workers were intellectuals who had studied in universities in Europe and who were now doing hard labor. And they were my friends, friends of my father, relatives, cousins. There were three or four priests among them, priests who had been arrested before our eyes and we could do nothing to help them. On the contrary, we had to tell them to go and dig ditches.

Now I work for a company that acts in the name of the government. It is a nation-wide company, and this is its branch in Shkoder. It uses government money and it has the authority to allocate apartments. We also check everything that the private companies build, the money they use, how they spend it, the quality of the construction. Last year we started to build about seven hundred apartments, and almost two hundred of them are already finished. We have been funded by the European Community and the World Bank. These seven hundred apartments are planned to be used not only by the persecuted people, but also by the homeless. Seven hundred is too few. All the families that have had at least one family member in prison or in exile for political reasons will get free houses forever, and it will be paid by the government. As for the homeless, they will receive no-interest loans from the government. Those who have had no home, and no one in prison either, will receive a government loan, but they will have to pay it back, without interest. While the others will have to pay for it. The government will decide who qualifies for receiving the no-interest loans. There are many homeless. I don't know how long it will take.

There are thirty thousand unemployed people in Shkoder. How many of them are homeless?

I don't know the answer to this question. It's not our office that deals with the problem of the homeless. It is an office in the City Hall, the office of the housing problems. For example, there are families that actually live in houses that belong to other people, and these houses have to be turned back to their owners because their property had been taken from them. There might be about one thousand such families. And some have lived crowded in a single room. For example, six families used to live in my house. They are all going to receive apartments, according to their requirements. They are going to get enough space for themselves.

My father used to tell me, forget the past, forget the past. I try to do that, but when I confront it everyday, it is impossible. If everybody were good now, it would be easier to forget. But we encounter the past in every step we take, every day. They come everyday, people who have been persecuted, and they ask "Have you received the funds from the bank, the funds to build the new apartments? Do you have funds to give us credit?" It is mainly people who have suffered in the past that come to our offices, because the communists have already bought their apartments, they have solved their housing problems. The smugglers, and the corrupt, those who earn a lot of money from their business, have also solved their housing problems. So it is the most honest and the poorest part of the population that comes and knocks at our doors, the part of the population who are not money-mongers. The honest part. It is impossible to forget. I get so desperate with their

problems that I feel like giving up. Nevertheless, it is a sin to compare the present to the past. It is a sin before God. It is absurd to be a pessimist today. I am optimistic for the future. But I am optimistic for the future of my kids, not for my own future. But the kids have started to neglect school. They spend too much time in front of the TV screen.

Are people angry about the present conditions?

No, in no way. This makes the situation more touching, because they understand. They are content with the changes.

Rozina Luli outside the Luli home, Shkoder.

I AM MARK KUSIA. I was born in 1953 in Dukagjin. I left Dukagjin when I was eighteen and I worked in the Hydrocentral for twenty two years. Thirteen years I worked underground. I have been jobless for four months. I have five children and I get thirty dollars per month for the family. My life is very difficult – I am living in a tunnel. Two families live in the same tunnel with many children. Our goal is to build a house, but we have nothing to build a house with. We cannot go abroad; how could we go? The main thing is to improve our economic situation. With the money we earn we won't be able to build a house in our lifetime. We are unemployed. Thirty dollars to keep five souls alive. The prices are very high and we cannot pay them. We try to get by and we try with all our strength to find a job, but where to find one? It is impossible. I have five brothers in the mountains in Dukagjin, with three acres of land. This is a brief summary of my life. We are waiting for the future, we do not know what to expect.

To love, to kiss, to embrace your children is not enough: they also need to eat. We are informed that Albania has received much aid. But we have seen none of it, and we cannot even find a place to raise our complaints, because nobody hears. Everybody has a deaf ear for us. The world is helping Albania but we are destroying things.

I am very deeply impressed by your visit to a very poor Albanian family. It is the first time that we have had visitors from abroad – or even from this country. We don't know how to reward you for that, and I will feel very much in debt to you for my entire life.

Opposite: *Mark Kusia and daughter in tunnel home, near Shkoder.*

M Y NAME IS LUIGJ NIKOLLE GECAJ. I was born in 1955. I live in Bajze. After the privatization laws were issued, I bought this cafe with six partners. The others have sold their shares.

How is business now, in 1994?

Good. Compared to 1991, the begining of Albanian business, if you call this a business, there are some difficulties: it is difficult to afford things, especially lately. The price of coffee has gone up to nine hundred leks. And you have to bear in mind that there are other things, too. You have to buy and sell Pepsi, Coca Cola, Yupi and other things with prices that are high, fifty leks for three hundred grams. In a word, we have reached European standards with our prices, while in other aspects we are still far behind.

Did you have any difficulties in buying this building?

The main problem was with the money. But also there were some debates, because the law was not stabilized and fixed at the time. The problem is that this place is considered holy, a "Center for a Log" place. It has been a place for people to gather on religious occasions for many many years, maybe five to six hundred years. Even in the documents and the maps it was considered a holy place. It has never been anyone's property. As it is a very important place, some people who have the support of people in the local government have created problems for us. We have appealed to the Constitutional Court in Tirane but they anulled that because the opposing side was not present, although we were the opposing side.

My profit is only enough for an average life under the present conditions in Albania. I think that our only hope is to pass from one day to another. There are no improvements.

Luigj Nikolle Grecaj outside his cafe, Bajze.

I AM AHMET OSJA, the headmaster of the "Haxhi Sheh Shamija" Medreseja School. There were schools of this kind in Shkoder years and years ago. Fifty years ago the religious schools were closed. Three years ago, when the mosques were opened, we returned to this ancient tradition of our people. At the same time, we took into consideration the society's development during these years. That is why we kept the general formation: we give scientific subjects together with religious subjects aiming to prepare religious cadres. At the same time, if a pupil prefers medicine or engineering, for example, he may go to the university. So, all the pupils have the same program as the other schools in Albania, plus religious subjects. They have six classes every day except Friday, when they have only four classes because the pupils of the middle form go to the main hall, to the mosque of our school, for the midday ceremony.

Ahmet Osja at graduation ceremonies, Medreseja School, Shkoder.

Some of the pupils are from Shkodra, and from the regions and villages near Shkoder. We also have students who come from regions outside Albania's borders. In fact they are Albanians, they speak Albanian, but they live in Montenegro or Kosove. The pupils are ten to fifteen years old. We accept students here only after we have tested them in some scientific subjects and in their general knowledge of the Islamic religion. At the end of each school year, the teachers prepare short comments on each student's performance and express their opinion as to where each of them is more likely to succeed, in religion or in other fields.

This school is different from Islamic schools in other countries. It takes into consideration the traditions of other peoples, as well as many other things that the Arabic peoples have. We are interested in economic and social development in general, the development of society. And, if this knowledge is far away – for example, if it is in China – we must go there to get it. At the same time, it must relate to the place and the time in which we live. For Islam, the believers of the other religions are brothers.

Our school was opened through the initiative of the citizens of Shkoder who prepared the school programs and teaching plans, who made all the arrangements and provided the material base. Though we have not completely secured the material base, we hope that gradually we will fulfill these needs. We hope that the pupils who graduate will eventually guide Islamic believers. They must do away with some phenomena that you may see in different people. But first we are dealing with many problems opening this school. It was not easy for us after fifty years.

Antoneta Luli, director of the Branko Kadia elementary school, Shkoder.

MY NAME IS ANTONETA LULI, I am thirty nine years old. I am married; my husband is teacher of physical education. I have two children, a daughter in the first grade and a son in the fourth. I studied mathematics and taught in villages for fifteen years. Now I am the director of a school in Shkoder. Every job is difficult, but the conditions in Albania at this time – there are many problems. For example my school is in a building whose owner wants it back. We must move and it's a project to build a new school. But I think we can stay in this building another year.

My school is really the best of Shkoder, as far as the level of pupils and the teachers is concerned. There are many parents who want to bring their children to my school but I don't even have enough room for the children from this part of town. But the place is in very bad condition.

You are the only woman we have met with an interest in politics. When did you become interested in being active politically?

The movement for democracy began in Albania in 1990. At that time I was a teacher in a village, and I and some of my friends were active in fighting against the communist system. I think politics is my passion. I don't know why, but I like to do something good, although people who like politics are not held in great respect in this society.

I am a member of the Democratic Party and of the Council of the Democratic Party for the District of Shkoder. We are twenty one in this council – there are only two women. It is the opinion of the council that women can help solve political problems. And I try; I will do it if I can. But I have many problems in the family, with the children, in the home. When democracy began in our country, many, many women fought for it; we were the first to fight. I remember the big meeting in the square: it was like a war at that time in Shkoder and the communist government used rifles and tanks in the city. The women were the first, then came the children and young people, and then the others. I think sometimes women are braver than men. I think women are very important for politics because they understand many problems. I think we must have free women – we must fight for the emancipation of women: if we don't have free women in Albania, we will have no emancipation for society, because the woman educates the family, the children. But I think in Albania we must emancipate the men first and then the women. The emancipation of women is difficult in Albania, because opinion is conservative. And for that, we must fight. For example, we will begin a new organization for women in the city. I think when women take part in different organizations they will do a good job for society, for family, for education, for everything, because women are less compromised, less corrupt.

Also we never see women in the cafes, but we see men there all day, drinking raki.

Yes, and this is while they are supposed to be on the job.

It's difficult, it's difficult, but I think now, and in the future, if the law is strong, everything will change for Albania. I think that for democracy to go ahead the law must be very strong. The Parliament is working on laws and the laws exist. But the people don't like to enforce them. I am very very much for enforcing the laws. If the government doesn't enforce the laws, democracy in Albania will be in danger.

There are people who think that democracy means to be free to do anything they like. I listen to many students who say now, "if we like, we will go to school, and if we don't, we won't." Their parents say that if this is democracy, they don't like it. Last year many parents talked about that problem and said the university should make rules for the students: for example, if you are absent for a certain number of days, then you are out. I understand that in a democracy rules are important. Democracy is to be free in the mind – to be free within rules. Democracy is not, for example, to go to your job when you want, and not when you don't. Democracy is discipline, I think.

I AM LIZA ZEFI, thirty nine years old. I have three boys. We don't have tools to till the land. We use tractors for which we pay. Other work, like hoeing and watering, is done by hand. We have a cow and two calves. We grow corn, wheat, melon, apples, tomatoes and cucumbers and so on, all sorts of vegetables. But they are just enough for the family. My husband works in town, as a baker. The other members of the family are unemployed. We used to live in a village near the lake Vau i Dejes. We built that house nine years ago; it was a big house. We were working inside it when it rained heavily and the hill near the house fell over it. And then the house slid down and cracked. We had to come here because it was dangerous to stay there at the foot of the hill. We bought this place here, at the time of the transition. We bought only the house, because the land belongs to someone who used to be in Shkoder, but we don't know where he is now. No one knows what will happen if he comes. If he doesn't come it will be okay.

Here when a man and a woman walk together, the man goes first and the woman follows behind him. And as you saw, Stan was the first to be served coffee by my sister. It is because of the *kanun* of Lek Dukagjini. It is still respected. According to the *kanun*, the woman must work inside the house while the men till the land or do other work outdoors. During communism it was said that women were equal to men. But after that the people started to respect the *kanun* much more than before.

We used to speak of equality before, and the woman had to work outdoors, as much as the man. And they got little money for the work they did, which made them totally unsatisfied. While now there are some who say that it is better for women, because they can stay home, they do the household work and no one shouts at them. Before there was the Party secretary and other members of the Party who used to control every move we made. While now we can stay home, take care of the kids, take care of the house and no one is telling us what to do.

It is beginning to change now; in the towns it is different. But here it is the *kanun*. The man is not a man if he mixes up with housework. In the mountains it is worse. The higher you go the worse it is.

Opposite: *Liza Zefi, Rrence.*

Tom Curraj, Bajze.

MY NAME IS TOM CURRAJ. I own a cafe in Bajze. Formerly I was an agronomist. I was in charge of the fruits and vegetables of the cooperative in Bajze and it was my duty to provide food for thirteen thousand people and to provide some of the varieties, like grapes, tomatoes, and watermelon, for export. Fifty percent of all the production was given to the government. We also produced medicinal herbs, about thirty to forty tons a year. We produced *raki*. So that was my work for eight years. Then I became chief agronomist and thirteen other agronomists were under my supervision. We grew corn, wheat, tobacco, livestock. We had a lot of land, about three thousand one hundred hectares, and we had four thousand one hundred workers. We produced about four thousand tons of wheat every year, about eight hundred tons of tobacco, three hundred tons corn – half of the corn was used for bread – and we produced milk. Then, in the last year, I started working as the chief of the agricultural cooperative – that was in 1990–1991. I was never a party member. Even now, I am not a member of any party. I sympathize with the democratic movement, but I am not a member of any of the political parties.

During my activity as chief, apart from the things I mentioned above, one of my priorities was to repair the roads of the village, which in the past were in such a bad state that even after a small rain you couldn't enter it. We were known in Shkoder as "The Village of the Red Mud." I eliminated this problem when I was the chief because I hated people from Shkodra making fun of us. Now the cars can move on our village roads every day of the year. This was my activity under the communist regime. Then we started a business, in order to survive. I bought this cafe some seven months ago, for twenty thousand dollars. I didn't have all the money, but I borrowed from friends and relatives. I employ eight people. I supply the goods for the cafe. The business is doing well. I am content. So I have decided to go on in this kind of business. Another aim I have, if the government ever helps me, is to get back to my speciality and build a greenhouse for producing vegetables.

What has happened to agriculture here?

It is in extremely bad condition: people are all involved in smuggling gas, because there is a lot more profit in it. And second, there is no water. We used to have a ditch that brought water from Lake Shkoder, close to the Yugoslav border. All this field was watered by the lake. When the land was distributed to the peasants, they each found a part of the ditch on their land. Some of them damaged their part. Also the commune [district] didn't take proper care of this problem, because they encountered a lot of difficulties. Today people have problems even with their drinking water. I was just in Hoti to get some water there and bring it here for my cafe. Water is the worst problem in this region.

Today it is very difficult to bring two or three people together, because I am dealing with my business, you might be doing something else, which might bring you much more money than the land. Only those who can do none of these other jobs are forced to work on the land, but they are not able to work on irrigation. The government has given money and the commune has appointed people to work on that, but they just take the money and do nothing but spend it in my cafe. So the water never comes. Many people have old mentalities, especially the older part of the population, and it adds to that when you say that in the past we used to have a lot of water while now, in the days of democracy, we don't even have drinking water. People have started to doubt, and not only to doubt, but also to want the old system back.

Dede Prendaj, chairman of the commune, district of Shale.

M Y NAME IS DEDE PRENDAJ; I'm thirty years old. I was born in Nenmavriq, in Shale, half an hour from Bregu i Lumit, on the right bank of the river. My family lives there – my mother, my father, five brothers and one sister. It would be a big family for American, but for Albanians it is normal. I am engaged to be married. I am the chairman of the commune of Shale. Shala has eleven villages and about seven thousand inhabitants. It is situated in the mountains, one hundred kilometers from Shkodra, close to the border with Yugoslavia. Agriculture and livestock are the main occupations of the people there, but there are some secondary ones, for example wood processing and some business in trade. I graduated in agronomy in 1988 from the University of Tirane and I worked in an agricultural cooperative for three years. When the democratic movement started, I was appointed the chairman of the multi-party council of the village. I was elected chairman of the commune two years ago. I have to solve all the problems arising in my area, economic, social, health, education, public order, etc. The main problem is the infrastructure; that includes the hospital too. The hospital was built fifty years ago. We are establishing connections with international charity organizations, for example Feed the Children. They are going to reconstruct the whole building and to reorganize the way the hospital is functioning. We also need to have some specialists here, because we have only two doctors. Even the village health center is going to undergo some reorganization. We cannot do it ourselves, because we are poor.

Until a year ago the hospital didn't have any car. Then a man from Kosova donated a Volkswagen that worked for some time, but it doesn't work now. When we have to take a patient to the hospital in Shkoder, we make use of cars that come through by chance. In the winter, when there is snow and the road is blocked, we have to carry them in our arms for four or five hours, like in World War II, and then try to find a truck to take them to the hospital.

How are the people of this region responding to the changes in the government and the changes in society?

The people of Shale love democracy and support it. Life is more colorful now. But to come out of that great poverty we have had, we need to work very hard.

Does the kanun of Lek Dukagjini still have an effect here? Do people still follow it?

It influences the life of the people, especially when it comes to tradition. In the time when the *kanun* ruled, it was the strongest constitution ever. But the law is the first to be respected. It is not a big problem today. Life has moved forward. Parts of the *kanun* have been abandoned. The chapter that deals with the role of women in the *kanun* is the one that has been most abandoned, because in the *kanun* the woman is treated like a working tool, not like a human being. The mentality has changed one hundred percent. According to the *kanun*, a woman who goes to the beach must be shot at once, but now women go to the beaches as much as they like.

[Translator: You have to change the men first! I say always the men – it's difficult to change them.]

For some problems, when no solution is found within the law, then the *kanun* might be used. In other cases, for example, if two people fight against each other over land, they prefer to follow the *kanun* rather than asking the police. Now there are problems in enforcing the law. In the past we were under a very severe dictatorship.

[Translator: Did you hear the rifles last night? It was terrible. People don't know the law; if they knew the law they wouldn't do that.]

It is just the law being too tolerant.

Maybe in Dukagjin there is a lot of tolerance.

We have some tolerance because we are one thousand meters above sea level. We are closer to God.

Are there any examples when the law says one thing and the kanun says another?

There are some cases. For example, in vengeance regulations, when blood is pardoned, the person who is pardoned is free, there are no further consequences. But according to the law he has to be put in prison. There are a lot of cases when people protect their friends, influenced by the *kanun.* If someone wants to kill somebody else, but that person is accompanied by a third one, it is difficult to kill him, because he is protected by this third one. If someone kills your enemy before you do it, you have to kill him. Also according to the *kanun,* the enemy cannot kill you when you are a guest in somebody's house, because the owner of that house protects you. Or, if your guest is killed while at your house, you have to take revenge for him. The *kanun* has its good sides too. *Besa,* for example.

If someone had shot us, would our host really have gone and shot him?

[Translator: I can't listen. I am Albanian and it is terrible.]

Yes, because it is very difficult for us to pardon. Though the law has its own influence, it is still difficult to set up law and order law here, in the mountains. To do it you would have to bring one policeman for each person.

We have seen Protestant missionaries coming into Theth. How do people respond to them?

There are some missionaries who try to do their work here. We welcome them and see them off. We have had no problems with them. We treat them as friends, as we are liberal. We are not afraid of these missionaries. Even Turgut Pasha wasn't able to change our religion.

Is there anything you'd like to tell us that we have not asked?

I think that this is a time when there are many problems to be solved in Albania. The people who take it on themselves to deal with these problems must be crazy.

So how did you make the decision to accept this responsibility?

I had never dreamt of working in such a position, but it was imposed on me. Maybe it is not good to speak well of yourself, but whenever I have worked I have done my job properly and people trusted me. This job is for four years; then there will be another election. I don't think I'll do this again; I have other plans. I'd rather study English than be the chairman of the village commune. I haven't yet decided what kind of work I want to do, but I'd like to study law. I am very fond of books and I don't like government business. If I weren't the chairman of the commune, I'd have been able to speak to you without a translator.

MY NAME IS RROK SMAJLAJ; I was born in Broja in 1961. I finished elementary and secondary schools in my village. I went to high school in Tamare and then I graduated from the University of Tirane, in biology. I have been teaching vertebrate zoology at the University of Shkoder for three years.

I am doing graduate study on the mammals of north Albania, especially those of the Alps. I have gathered a lot of materials for some particular species: *Sciurus vulgaris, Talpa europea, Rupicapra rupicapra, Canis lupus,* [see glossary] etc. I catch some of them with small traps I have in my house. I put pieces of meat in the traps, fruits, and leave them in forests or meadows. We ask people like shepherds or others who work in the mountains where such animals might be, how they can be found, where to look for them. We also look for the different signs they leave, such as tracks, manure, lairs. Some are caught in other ways, maybe not the right ways, like shooting at them, as happens with foxes, wolves, etc. My object is to study the system of mammals of this area and their bioecology (their living conditions, their behavior, etc.) We don't have any study of this kind in our country, and that is the reason I have chosen it. It has been approved by our biology department, as well as the university. I am also connected with the University of Bologna, Italy. I cooperate with people there and in Austria and elsewhere.

Rrok and Ardiana Smajlaj, Lepushe.

MY NAME IS ARDIANA SMAJLAJ, I was born in 1968. I finished primary school in Vukeil, not here in Lepushe, and I finished my studies in Shkoder. When I was a student I dreamed of being an actress or a dancer. I studied with artistic groups in high school and at the university. I took part in some performances. But then I came up against hard reality; I became a teacher because there were greater possibilities for jobs. I have been teaching for three years. First I taught here, in the school that was destroyed. Now I am working in a village outside of Shokder. My work is interesting, my students are clever, and they are nice, if I may say so. But the conditions in my school are very bad, without enough books, without pencils, it's terrible. I buy pencils for the students with my own money. My salary is forty dollars a month. The teachers everywhere in Albania are dissatisfied with this salary. It is not enough to live on, especially in the cities. In the country it is different because they have animals, they have land to grow food, cabbage, tomatoes. We can't do that in the city.

MY NAME IS SOKOL ZHAB-JAKU. I graduated from the University of Tirane, in the faculty of medicine, five years ago. I worked for three years in Tamare and Vermosh in the mountain zone – a very difficult zone. Now I am working in a village about seven miles from Shkodra. My profession is very difficult, and there are a lot of problems. In general, we need everything, because the people are very poor, and we doctors are very poor in materials.

The main problem is obtaining medicine. Now there are private pharmacies in Albania, and the prices are very high. So it is very difficult for people to buy the drugs and to recover. The pharmacies of the state are very poor in drugs because the privatized pharmacies are more powerful than the state ones.

Medical care in Albania is free, just as it was under the socialist system. But now the patient feels an obligation to the doctor – he wants to pay. It is not required, but in reality, everyone knows that to recover one needs some money. But for people who do not have money, I think for the doctors it does not matter. For example, in surgery a doctor cannot distinguish between a rich man and poor man. After the operation a rich man can pay more, a poor man can pay less. People pay usually thirty or forty dollars for an appendicitis. That may seem a low sum, but the salary of the doctors

Dr. Sokol Zhabjaku, Shkoder.

is only fifty or sixty dollars per month. So, doctors are very satisfied with this payment, and now they work a lot.

I work in a little room, not even a clinic. There are two doctors working in my village, and there are nurses not only in the village center, but in every quarter of the village. All the babies are vaccinated. It is considered a great failure if a baby is not vaccinated, and it is very rough for the nurses if they do not vaccinate a baby. It was the law of the socialist system, and now again.

There are many people with rheumatism. Albania is very rich in water – the water is one of the factors that causes rheumatism. I think even the culture, the magical culture, is one of the factors that causes this. For example, there is a river near here, the Drini, whose water is very very cold. But people always bathed in the Drini although it was very very dangerous for them. Another factor is the suffering of the people. For example, under the dictatorship the people of the village had to worked in the fields, in the rain, without shoes, all day long. It was impossible for us to help. It was mainly the girls who worked in the fields. The rare foreigners who came here years before saw only girls working in the fields and they were all surprised. Now everyone works when he wants and when he needs to. They still work very hard. But the conditions are not the same.

We would like to ask you about the health care in the mountains. We were very surprised, for example, to learn that so many families had lost a young woman, a daughter, mother of the children. We asked why and nobody gave a clear answer. They said, "well, bad blood."

I think one of biggest problems in Vermosh, in Tamare, and in Selce is the culture of the people. The mothers, especially the new mothers, do not know how to raise babies. Sometimes I gave them some lessons – how to take care of the baby, how to feed the baby, and so on, but not all the mothers were attentive. For example, one mother fed her baby only water with sugar. She told me that the baby was beautiful and growing well. She did not understand the importance of the mother's milk and other substances that the baby needs. You have seen that in Lepusha and Vermoshi, the people and the houses are very clean. But about the babies, they need more culture.

Hemorrhages are the main reason young mothers die. It is very difficult to stop hemorrhaging. In the city of Shkoder, all the mothers go to the hospital to give birth, but in the villages they give birth at home. The main reason babies die is dyspepsia, bad nutrition. This is, as I said, from the poor culture of the mother and the family. I have sent some cases to Shkoder – there is a hospital especially for the babies who are suffering from poor nutrition here, and they have saved them.

The structure of our villages is part of the problem – for example, there are a lot of houses far away from each other. When a baby is born, the doctor cannot stay every time, because he must attend to a lot of other problems. They do not have an ambulance. When I worked in the mountains four or five years ago, I could phone from Tamara or Vermoshi for an ambulance, with difficulty, but the ambulance arrived. Now the phones don't exist any more and so it's very difficult to get help to the patients. The dictatorship did some good things. The nurses went from home to home to visit the babies until they were one year old. If a baby died, the nurse was punished very, very, severely. Even the secretary of the party was concerned with this problem. Maybe he was ignorant, but he did not want any baby to die. It was the duty of the party; there was a slogan. After one year there was no longer special care. But for me and the other doctors, the patient is always the patient, whether it is a baby or a grownup. We ought to give the same care.

Patient, Dukagjin Hospital.

Lepushe cemetery,
overlooking village
center.

Lepushe, "Pearl of the Alps"

Diary Excerpts.

LEPUSHE is hard to find on the map, and if you were to glance at it from the back of one of the old trucks that rumble through, there would not seem to be much reason to stay, or even to stop there. The "center" is desolate: a little truckstop cafe, a very small, poorly-stocked store, and a tiny elementary school face a soccer field with no grass. Lepushans have not given thought yet to recycling – aluminum cans, unknown a few years ago, are tossed about on the ground.

But if you walk a few yards down the road from the center, you begin to understand why Lepushe is called "the pearl of the Alps." We could easily imagine that we were in Switzerland: the lush pastures, the high mountains, the rushing brooks, the wildflowers, the boulders. The handsome, widely-scattered houses are made of wood and stone; the roofs are weathered wood shingles. The summer air is fresh and cool, and the nights are crisp. The early mornings and early evenings, when the sheep are led up to higher pastures and when they are brought back down, are village social hours.

We were privileged to live in Lepushe for over two weeks as guests of the Grishaj family: Katrina and Zef, their two unmarried children, Pellumb and Flora, and Zef's elderly parents. Two older daughters are married: Ana Pepaj, with whose family we stayed in Selce, and Ardiana Smajlaj, who was visiting her parents with her husband Rrok while we were there. Diana (as she is called) and Flora lead much more modern lives than their sister. Although the older members of the family spoke only Albanian, communication was never a problem. Diana had taught herself English and spoke it quite well, Rrok and Flora could manage in English if necessary, and Pellumb was fluent in Russian (sometimes Stan's Italian or my rudimentary Albanian were also called into service).

Life is difficult everywhere in the Malesi e Madhe. Like their neighbors, the Grishajs do not have indoor plumbing, or refrigeration, or indeed a machine of any kind; they cook on woodstoves and, in the summer, on the open hearth in a shed. They spin wool from their sheep and then knit or weave it, they milk their cows for milk, butter, yogurt, and cheese, and all the agriculture is also done by hand. Just before we arrived, wolves attacked and killed one of the Grishaj's two cows. The family's only transportation is a single horse. The winters are long and cold, with winds and storms and six feet of snow, so the summers must be spent preparing for the winters. During the time that we were there, most of the people in Lepushe were occupied with haying. Both Zef and Katrina worked continually from dawn to dark. Everything is done properly in the Grishaj household – sanitation, hygiene, food preparation, animal care. It is model of enlightened mountain life.

During our days in Lepushe, we visited neighbors and friends of the Grishajs in nearby villages. In the evenings, we usually sat in the living room, watching television (the Grishajs have a satellite receiver) and talking with the family. On the evening of the World Cup finals, neighbors gathered in the small living room to cheer for the Italian team; one small boy was nearly distraught with grief when it lost. One evening Katrina dressed for us in her national (traditional) costume, in which she had been married. It is only worn for weddings and other special occasions; the last time she wore it was ten years ago, when she and some other women of the village were invited to Tirane to play bit parts in a film called "Street of Liberty." (Diana didn't wear it for her wedding; like many Albanian brides today, she wore a white dress.) A few evenings later, Katrina, Diana, and Flora dressed me up in Katrina's costume – to the great amusement of all of us – and then Flora put it on for the first time. The grandfather played his *lahute* for us and sang old songs; we recorded them but later, in Shkoder, an Albanian musicologist told us that because of the grandfather's advanced age, he could not make out the words.

At the very end of our stay, late in July, there was a big festival in the center of Lepushe in honor of Saint Premtja. Religious festivals, banned during the communist years, are being revived again now. People came from all over Malesi e Madhe – by that time we had met many of them and it was a pleasure to see so many friends. The mass, led by Archbishop Robert Ashta, was sung in a responsive chant, using only two or three tones – the most ancient Albanian music, strange to our ears but unforgettably beautiful. Singing the mass in this way is unique to the northern mountains: in Shkoder the service is much like everywhere else in the world. Afterwards there were picnics. We found ourselves next to a group of men who had roasted a sheep for the occasion, and had brought along bread, cheese, *raki* and rifles to make the celebration complete. Cupping hand to ear, they began to shout in a way that, we were told, was used in the past to broadcast news from mountaintop to mountaintop. Indeed, travelers in this region early in this century reported that by this method news could travel all the way to Shkoder in only a few hours. Now that there is no longer mail service to the mountains, and the telephone lines have been destroyed, perhaps this custom too will be revived.

Opposite: *Katrina Grishaj wearing her national dress.*

Katrina Grishaj chopping wood outside cookhouse.

Zade Grishaj knitting socks.

Sharpening scythes.

Cutting grass for hay.

Gystina Grishaj and
Ndue Dragu moving hay.

Ardiana Smajlaj washing clothes.

*Archbishop Robert Ashta leading
the mass, Saint Premtja Festival.*

Saint Premtja Festival.

Celebrating Saint Premtja
Festival in traditional style.

Leaving Lepushe.

CHAPTER FOUR

LONG LIFE TO YOUR CHILDREN!

Jetë të gjatë fëmijëve tuaj!

Early evening stroll, Shkoder.

"I Like Very Much to Hear the Songs in English"

A rash statement to make, and yet I venture to make it, is that Scutari, from the point of view of costume, must be the most picturesque and dramatic town in Europe. The streets of Scutari itself are merely backgrounds – the main street full of insignificant houses, many of which are painted with pleasant and garish tints; the subordinate streets are merely alleys between high walls, with great gateways . . . But the populace . . . Of women's costume there were at least eight wholly different varieties. — Jan and Cora Gordon, "Two Vagabonds in Albania," 1927.

RELATIVELY SPEAKING, the Gordon's statement may still be true. One no longer sees eight wholly different varieties of women's dress, but many women, especially older ones living in nearby villages, continue to prefer their traditional clothes, with brightly colored hand-woven aprons and headscarves with intricate embroidery. Today the crowds in the streets of Shkoder form a kaleidoscopic pattern of traditional and modern, including some costumes the Gordons never saw: many young girls now wear shorts and short skirts, some of them very short. "Every outfit represents a fight with a mother," explained a sixteen year old friend, in English.

In High Albania the traditional family structure is evolving toward one with more autonomy for its individual members, but very slowly, in geological time. Older and younger generations may soon find themselves on a collision course as young people try to calibrate their lives with those of their contemporaries elsewhere.

For the world has arrived in what was until so recently the most isolated country in Europe, or at least the image of the world conveyed by foreign visitors, diplomats, business people, aid workers and other advisors, consumer goods, and television images. And it has arrived massively and all at once. The government still controls all Albanian radio and television, but today Albanians can feast on a rich diet of media junk food. Albanian television features old Hollywood swashbucklers and MTV, lavishly interpolated with Western commercial advertising (the only objections we heard to this advertising were that it wasn't Albanian-made and didn't promote Albanian products). With a satellite dish one can also watch sports, soap operas, horror movies, violent crime programs, pornography, idiotic quiz shows, and biased news from Italy, Turkey, Serbia, Montenegro, Tunisia, Greece, Egypt, and beyond. No one seemed to be concerned about the impact of this media blitz on Albanian society.

Political arguments are public now, although the government is rather prickly about media criticism. In 1992, there were only a few newspapers in Albania; in 1994 there are nearly as many newspapers as there are political parties (approximately thirty). Some newspapers are dedicated to sports, some to pornography, but most are the voice of one or another political group. Radio is also popular, and Radio Shkoder has a lively young staff that seeks out and reports the local news. (An interview with Stan was broadcast soon after he arrived in June.) Albanians are very eager to talk with visitors; it is hard to find a young person who is not studying English.

Newspaper stand, Shkoder. But this does not mean that the young believe that the future is in their hands. It is one of the easy cliches of reporting on the formerly communist countries of Europe that young people are adapting to their rapidly changing society with much more alacrity than their parents and grandparents. In the case of Albania, at least, the situation is more complex. Some young people see new opportunities emerging, but others are dismayed by, even fleeing from, Albania's poverty, high unemployment rates, and widespread corruption. Many older people are distressed by these things too, but others insist that freedom, especially the freedom to practice religion, is worth any social price. In short, there are younger as well as older pessimists, and older as well as younger optimists. (The people we spoke with all readily classified themselves as either optimists or pessimists: no one declared themselves to be both, though that would have seemed most reasonable to us.)

Mother and daughter, Shkoder market.

*Carrying the bride's belongings
to her new home, Grope.*

A Mountain Wedding

Diary Excerpt.

O NE AFTERNOON late in July, we attended the wedding of Shpresa Keraj and Peter Pellumbaj, the only doctor in the entire Malesi e Madhe. The village where his family lives is not far from Lepushe, on the road to Selce. The truck let us off on the road within sight of the house, and we walked across a ravine/river bed and up the hill to the wedding. The festivities were held outdoors, as is the custom. We sat at long wooden tables covered with back issues of the newspaper *Koha Jone*; an area in the middle of the courtyard was kept clear for dancing. After awhile the bride and her family arrived. First we saw some men of the family carrying her belongings up the hill to the house – clothes, rugs, some furniture. Then we heard singing and rifle shots, coming from the cluster of the people with her. Finally we saw her, magnificent and resplendent in the national costume, veiled, adorned with pearls, jewels, embroidery, scarves. Every detail was spectacular and classical.

The bride disappeared into the house and the music and dancing began. The music wasn't live – instead, they had excellent sound equipment. It was a mixture of traditional and rock, as was the dancing. It was beautiful to watch: many of the dancers, including our good friend Rrok Smajlaj, were very accomplished. Even tiny children joined in, doing their best to imitate the graceful motions of the dancers' hands. We would have liked to try it too, but we were too self-conscious.

There was lots of food, and lots of *raki* (served in beer bottles and continuously refilled), and a great many pistol and rifle shots. One woman at our table had a pistol in her purse; she and a friend kept taking it out and shooting it off. But most of the shooters were men who kept the pistols tucked into their waistbands. The bride came out and was guided from table to table (always looking down, even after her veil had been removed) as people sang traditional songs to her.

Shpresa disappeared into the house again and the dancing continued. Some people got drunk. As the dancing, drinking and shooting went on and on, Stan and I grew increasingly nervous. Suddenly the hosts decided that we all had to leave, in order to get the drunken guests out of there before someone got hurt. So the bride came out – with eyes still downcast – to say goodby, or rather to be said goodby to. I felt badly that things had ended this way, but when we got back to the road I heard the music start up again; I guess the relatives had stayed on and the party continued. People piled into vehicles (trucks, a van, and even a car or two) and drove off, oblivious to the dangers of driving while drunk. Indeed, Albanians seem to have no consciousness of danger on the road.

Opposite: *The bride wore the traditional dress of Malesi e Madhe.*

Above: *Friends and relatives dance.*

Rrok Smajlaj dancing.

*The bride is led from
table to table as guests
sing her praises.*

*Bride and groom
with relative.*

Above: *Conversation and stories.*

Following page: *Celebrating the marriage.*

191

Faces and Voices

the elusive future

Mayor Filip Guraziu continues:

WE PLAN TO ORGANIZE two centers in the town of Shkoder. One of them will be the square in front of this building – you can see it from here – and the other center will be at the park in front of the big cafe. I hope that they will be finished within this year. We have a problem, because if the state gives funds to build something it doesn't give any money to support the project itself. And so we have agreed that the company that builds will also pay for the project. We have been able to achieve some positive results with three different projects: restoring the old city hall, building the new marketplace with funds received from the World Bank, and rebuilding the park. We are going to build a very beautiful marketplace in the northeastern part of the town, not far from here, close to the music school. There are private companies that are going to invest in it. In a similar way we hope to start constructing a trade and tourist center near the Buna River. I happen to have some pictures of the old town here. Are you interested in seeing them?

[Translator: You are running late.]

(To the translator. We are not discussing whether I am late or not. We are discussing whether they are interested or not. They are our guests now and we have to help them.)

Today we are somewhat isolated from the rest of the country. The road from Tirana to Shkoder is narrow. In the past there used to be a large movement of goods and animals from Albania to Yugoslavia. Now the embargo against Yugoslavia has closed the border. The only way to develop the city is to turn the Buna into a navigable river, as it was in the past. It is only in this way that we'll be able to attract tourists to the city of Shkoder, bring them from the sea, through the river into the town. We think that under the castle, where a new park has been built, it would be good to build a center similar to the old one that existed in the 18th century, in order to be able to sell handicraft works there. This center should be surrounded by shops and service places of a similar nature. In this way we would restore one of our old traditions, close to a small port, which would be the port on the Buna River. The tourists coming from the sea will be able to leave their ships here, have a look at the handicraft shops, have their lunch in the restaurants of the city, and visit the castle. And if they like, they can go across the lake to Montenegro.

MY NAME IS GJELOSH DODE ASHTA. My wife's name is Shkurte and my daughter's name is Flora. I am twenty nine, my wife is twenty two and my daughter is a year and a half. I am from Dukagjin, from a mountain village called Falaj. I came to Shkoder in 1990 because it was very difficult for us to live there. Our main problem was that we didn't have land. I came here with nothing at all, and started working with a government-owned company. After the democratic changes, most of the workers were dismissed and left on welfare. After twelve months I had to work wherever I could. Sometimes I have been involved in the black market.

Gjelosh Dode Ashta with his daughter Flora, Shkoder.

Grinding rice stalks at the
Maize and Rice Research
Institute, Shkoder.

MY NAME IS ILIA LEKA, I am a chemical engineer and the head of the Chemical Laboratory of the Maize and Rice Research Institute. Our institute was established in 1971; it is the only one of its kind in Albania. It is dependent on the Ministry of Agriculture. It had about seven hundred hectares and about three hundred workers; we produced enough to fulfill the demands from all over the country. Now we have only fifteen hectares in all. Before we did a lot of analyses, but now there are only three of us here in this lab. At the beginning we were inexperienced – we had no means or apparatus with which to work. But in time we gained experience, without any help from abroad. We received some apparatus from Hungary, and we tried to set it up and work by ourselves. We did our best during those years. After democracy was established in our country, my colleague and I had the opportunity to go to Hungary for eight months to study *in vitro* cultivation and electrophoresis. But when we came back here, we had a lot of difficulties with the new director of the institute. For

Ilia Leka and Zhaneta Miloti in their laboratory.

example, he asked us, "What is electrophoresis? I don't know what it is." We continue to have a lot of difficulties, but we try to do our best. If we want to survive, we will have to have some connections with foreign institutes; otherwise this institute will be closed. Our lab, especially, must have connections with other labs to learn new methods and everything else. It is very difficult alone. The director of the institute doesn't care about it.

MY NAME IS ZHANETA MILOTI; I am a biochemist. We have two telephones here at our institute, but the lines were cut because we could not pay the one hundred fifty dollar tax for the phone. How can we be connected with other institutions without having at least a phone, not to mention a fax or other things? I have had the good fortune to go to Belgium, to visit other laboratories there, and I have been in Austria, France, Holland, and some other countries. I had a good offer to stay there and work. But because I have worked here for fifteen years, and because I love my country, I felt obliged to return and serve this institute. But when I came back here it was impossible; it was even worse than I feared.

I AM ARBEN ZAJMI, I am thirty years old. I work at the local radio station as a journalist. I deal with news programs, mostly, and I conduct interviews. I also plan historical, sport, socio-logical, and several other kinds of programs. Mostly I work with the news, world news, local news. I work at the television with the teletext and I take some news in French and Italian from television from abroad, but unfortunately, our television doesn't function very well.

I haven't been working here very long – only one year. I graduated from high school in 1982 and I studied in the workers' course for nine months, and after that I took a job in a factory and had a lot of other jobs. I was a shoemaker, a fireman, and a coachman (I drove coaches with a horse). But I passed a competition for this job. And I am really content because these last years I have been able to write in the newspapers to help democratic changes. Like a lot of young people, I felt a duty to help my country. I think broadcasting is a good means for emancipating the people.

I am interested mostly in the bad points of our present situation, because I think that's what we need to discuss at the moment. And our listeners agree. We have some programs with phone-in calls in direct broadcasting to give to the people a chance to share their opinions about the government, about work, about the corruption, about the state, about business, and several other things.

People call in, and most of them feel comfortable about talking. But a few of them still feel a little afraid because it used to be really dangerous.

Our station is an official one and we try to preserve, as far as possible, the liberty to do our work. At this time it is not difficult to do that, because I belong to the generation that was raised in the dictatorship, and if I wasn't scared before I have no reason to be scared now. But I am not always objective because that can cause damage or make troubles. I think we must be careful about that. In general, we like to criticize, but we are not in opposition to our government because we are paid by this government. By luck, we have a director who was a persecuted person: he's a brave man and he's not scared, he is not afraid of the authorities. So, we are going on with our job. I have thought about what I will do after this job, but it's not a problem for the moment. We haven't had any complaints.

Can the people who live in the mountains and are very isolated with no mail or telephone hear the radio station?

Yes, most of them can hear the radio station, but it depends on the atmospheric conditions. The station has a range of one hundred kilometers – our programs can be heard even beyond our borders.

How did you learn English? You speak very well.

I began to learn English three years ago. I learned by myself – I studied with a teacher for only a few months. I had no means to pay a teacher, so I bought some cassettes and books and I went on with my studies. When I worked at the factory I used to put on headphones and listen to the cassettes all through the day. And so I lived, in a figurative way, in an English environment. I listened to English until my ears were tired. I used to watch films and listen to the English programs of the radio stations such as the Voice of America or the BBC, or the Voice of Germany, the Voice of France, Radio Moscow.

At first when I began to learn English the principle reason was to be able to talk to people who came here from abroad, to tell them about the dictatorship, etc. Another reason was that I wanted to read Shakespeare and several other writers in the original because I am very fond of literature. I am studying languages and literature at the university, so I understand much more than the others – the general, the common people – about languages. English has some patterns that I haven't found in any other language, even in Albanian. For example, there is a special vocabulary, a syntactic one with a lot of uses for a word. And so that makes English sometimes really simple and sometimes really difficult. English is something deep that is really difficult at the basis.

Arben Zajmi in his office, Radio Shkoder.

Like all Albanians, I love my country. I had opportunities to go abroad, but I stayed here because I thought I should help my country. I think that our democracy is taking many steps forward. But, at the same time, we find a lot of difficulties. The most difficult thing in our way is the old mentality. Even the persecuted people – the people against the dictatorship – have a communist mentality. The best way to build our country is to give up this mentality and have an up-to-date one. My hope is in the new generation – in the school system. And through the school we can fight against corruption. Our future will be, of course, better – better than now.

*Tahir and Elpid Myftia,
Shkoder.*

I AM TAHIR MYFTIA and I am forty years old. After I finished high school, I continued my studies in Shkoder, in mathematics and physics. I worked for eleven years as a teacher in Shllak, which is at the top of the mountains, about eighty two kilometers from here. It's close to the hydropower station of Koman. There is no car road for a good part of the way. I used to go home only once a month. I taught in a very small school of forty students altogether and in very terrible conditions. The classrooms had no windows and rain leaked from the ceiling.

After eleven years there, I spent six years in another village which was far from here too. I traveled to school every day in buses which were in very bad condition. The school was larger and had more students. Then I came back to Shkoder. Now I am an Inspector of the School Board of the District of Shkoder.

Your family boasts a long line of religious leaders. Did you feel the desire to follow in their footsteps?

I have a great respect for them and I am proud of them. But I have taken another course in my life and it is not my concern to follow in the traces of my ancestors, though I respect people who do that.

Hatina Myftia, Shkoder.

I AM HATINA MYFTIA, I am thirty two years old. After finishing high school I went to the university to study construction engineering. I used to work as a technologist in a factory, but the factory has been closed. The workers were dissatisfied because they thought that they were working a lot more than they were paid. The factory closed because we had no money to pay the workers or to buy raw material. Now I am living on welfare, with the minimum pay of twenty dollars a month. This is very little money, because we have a child. I would like to buy a dress, but we must think twice before deciding to buy one. I am very happy when my husband buys me a dress, but we must spend our money for things that are more essential in our lives. When we decide to buy something we have to save money in order to do that. And we have to save for our daily bread and milk. But I am an optimist, because things are going to change for the better in the future. They have already changed, in a way. People here didn't use to have cars or color TVs.

I think that the lives of women are going to change when the economy improves. If I had modern equipment in the house, my life would be better. But as it is now, I have to handwash all the clothes, I have to spent a lot of time sewing socks and other things, because I have no money to buy new ones.

We notice that very few husbands do any cooking or cleaning. In America many families share the work. Is that changing here?

In our country the custom has been that husbands didn't help their wives. For example, my husband helps me but only in some simple things. I have to do the washing, the cleaning, the cooking. I must take care of the child. My husband takes a little care of the child too and sometimes does some shopping. I think that women in our country have had very difficult lives. Actually there are some slight changes, though there is still a difference in the treatment of women here and abroad and this is because of the prevailing old mentality. It will change, because now we are in touch with other countries and many people from abroad, from the United States, Germany, come here. Our husbands, seeing the others, will reflect that in one way or another.

Dawn, Lepushe.

A Mountain Family

DAUGHTER. I have told you about some relatives we have in the United States: they are three brothers and this land had belonged to their father. They have been there about thirty years; they own restaurants and some cafes there. They want to have this land back, and this house even though we built it; they have told us that they want it in memory of their father, to use during the summer. This is something really terrible for us and makes us very unhappy.

FATHER. I cannot agree to that. There is no way for me to give them my house unless they build me a house somewhere else. But they wouldn't do it and I have no means at all to build a new house now, with today's high prices. I cannot buy land and build a house.

DAUGHTER. They came last year and told us to go, to leave the house within a year. And we are thinking about what to do. It is a big problem, a real problem. Because they are our relatives, we thought we could settle this without asking the help of the government. But the facts are different, quite different. Let's hope we won't need to ask the government's help.

Isn't it government policy to protect the people who are living on the land?

DAUGHTER. Yes, of course. But I have told you the government is hopeless. The law must be respected above everything else. Sometimes we feel powerless in a poor country and most of the time we don't know what we are going to do.

FATHER. I don't want my son to do what I have done in life. I don't want him to build a new house. Another time has come now. He has to follow his own way in life. It is difficult for him to do well in the city, but even here we are deprived of the land, and maybe even the house. It's very difficult; who knows what will happen? After all, it is the strongest that makes the law.

A Pensioner in Shkoder

MANY PEOPLE ASK ME whether I have had any rewards or any profits from democracy. Look at what I am wearing! These last two years they have started to build two new apartment buildings. I knocked only once at the door of the housing office, because I feel ashamed to go and keep asking them. I also made a written application. I spoke to the chairman of the Circuit Committee and also to the mayor and all I asked was, as they have given my daughter an apartment in one of those buildings, would they find the possibility of putting me there too; I would exchange this apartment for that one. The reply was that they had already distributed all the apartments, which wasn't true. I think, based on what someone who has a very high position said when I explained my situation, there is corruption here, great corruption. You have to have money. But where can I find money, with twenty five dollars a month?

I wanted to go and live close to my daughter for two reasons: first, she has three children, and I want to be close to my grandchildren. The second reason is for me and my wife when I will no longer be able to look after myself. They didn't want to hear. The only person who has shown some signs of respect was today. He passed close to me and stopped. He had previously worked with a horse cart; now he was driving a car. His name is Kim. He stopped the car and asked if he could help me and see me to my house. That is life.

Kujtim Gjelaj, Lepushe.

MY NAME IS KUJTIM GJELAJ. I was born in Albania, in the village of Brej. I am twenty six years old. I left my country together with one hundred people in December, 1990. It was very cold, there was snow and very bad conditions. When we arrived across the mountains, the Yugoslav army caught us. We were interviewed; I said my father had been in prison and my family was in a very bad condition because the regime was very very bad. I was sent to a refugee camp for about two years and seven months. It was very bad in the camp. Afterward we went to a hotel, it was better than the camp. I stayed in Belgrade for three years. I did not have any means to go to another country. Then they sent me back here. My family is very poor. We are ten children. Five sisters, five brothers, my mother and father. I have no grandfather or grandmother. We don't have work. So here I am, without a future. It is a very difficult life here in the mountains.

Do you think about moving to a city, to Shkoder or Tirane?

What could I do there? I have no job there, I have nobody there, what can I do there? It is impossible – they have too many people, and nobody works. I think just of leaving. I need to go to another country to work. I can do anything, but I have no job.

What are your thoughts about the future of Albania? How it might change?

It is very difficult to change life in the mountains. Maybe in the cities some things will change, but it will take a long time. What can change here? What will happen? Nothing. After one hundred years, it will be the same as now.

MY NAME IS KRISTINA MIRUKU. I am twenty seven years old and I am married; I have a son, three and a half years old. I graduated as an English teacher at the University of Tirane. I taught English for three or four years and then I started work as an interpreter with an English project for mentally handicapped people. The project has three main aspects. One is community work, another is running a course for training staff to work with people with mental handicaps, and the third aspect is the parents' association. They are trying to help parents to develop their own association, to run it, to manage to solve problems and things like that. This is nearly a new culture for us. Until now mentally handicapped people have been treated only medically. Now they are trying to input the new idea, the new view.

How would you describe the new view?

Treating them as part of the community. Treating them like everybody else. I am speaking about mentally handicapped children, not mentally ill persons. We go to the doctor when we are ill and we need medical care. Mentally handicapped children don't need so much medical care, but they need affection and everything else that other people need in their lives. With the English project there has been a physiotherapist visiting them, telling them how to do exercises. And lately, they have had an orthopedist, not a proper chiropodist, but somebody who can make shoes for children with disabilities, with problems with their feet. Just usual help and advice; the families, nurses, and other staff in these institutions get advice from the English workers.

Where does the money for this project come from?

Mencap – for people with mental handicaps, and other foundations like Body Shop. They make soap and body cream, and things like that. Some funds come from the European Community as well.

Do you find that people are eager for new ideas, or are they resistant to them when it comes to this issue?

Well, we have to face different attitudes. Some are quite eager to have these new ideas and learn more about the children. For example, we see families that until now have kept their children at home. They didn't want others to know that they had a mentally handicapped child; it was a shame for them. Now we see them taking the children out in their wheelchairs. So, something is changing. And at the beginning, the English volunteers and workers found it difficult to get the parents together to make new teams and take minutes and things like that. But, they are quite different now. They are having their own meetings and they are having their elections.

Their main problem for the moment is to find a good school for the children with mental handicaps, with learning difficulties, because their present school is together with the mainstream school. This is not good and appropriate for the children. For two years now they have been trying to find a new place. Apparently they have found a place, but they need more funding and new equipment for the school. That has been their main problem. They are also trying to help other families that are in financial difficulties. They have been funded by a Muslim organization which has promised to provide funding for orphaned mentally handicapped children and some families who couldn't pay their taxes when their houses were made private properties. Some families could not afford that. Now they have just had a concert in the Shkoder theater with children with learning difficulties and other people with mental illnesses. The children played, sang, and recited. The theater was full and it was very good.

Things are beginning here.

Yes, private business a lot, but not voluntary work.

Do you like the work that you are doing?

Yes. I even started reading about mental handicaps, in addition to the translations I did. If we hadn't had this chance to work with this project we would never learn anything about it. At the

*Kristina Miruku,
Shkoder.*

beginning it was quite difficult for us to make a distinction between mental handicap and mental illnesses. I have been using the books that they have in the office, they have a small library of books.

How do you see your own career developing?

In September I am starting a new job, teaching phonetics at the English department opening at the University of Shkoder. It will be a new experience and will be a lot of work, much effort. I will have to study about this field. I would also like to know more about mental handicaps, the special needs of children with learning difficulties; it's very interesting. I am trying to decide what I am going to do next.

What does your husband do?

He is a mechanic; at the moment he is working in Italy. He has just gone. Maybe he will be back by Christmas time. Maybe I can get a tourist visa just to go and see him.

MY NAME IS ARBEN ZENELI, I am twenty five years old. I was born in Shkoder, and I finished the high school for music in 1987. After that I worked in the same school as a teacher, for five years. Then there was a reorganization of the school, because there were fewer pupils. It was impossible to give work to all the teachers that were in the school. I was the first to be let go. The other teachers had more experience.

Why were there fewer students?

Because they were not interested in learning music any more. This school does not offer good prospects for an Albanian. The pupils can't give concerts because interest in music is declining. They can only be music teachers and the possibilities for that are very few. My friends and I used to give concerts here in school or in the theater. I like to play Beethoven, Scarlatti, Chopin . . . But interest in classical music is very low here now. In Tirane it is quite different because there are more people interested in classical music, and there are many shows, operas, many ballets.

Shkoder is well known for its composers. This school is named after a great composer from Shkodra, Preng Jakova. But all these composers, now and before, finished school in Tirane or in Moscow and then returned to Tirane to work. This is the reason that Tirana is more musically rich. The composer for piano, Tonin Harapi, died two years ago. He was a very able composer. He studied in Russia. And also Çesk Zadeja studied in Russia. In their music we can always find the motifs of the songs of Shkoder. That is very good because now we no longer sing or listen to folk music. When we play their music on the piano we can remember it again.

So Tirana is rich in composers, while Shkodra is poorer and has few people who are able to do this work. We needed teachers for the university conservatory, so Tirana sent a teacher here. She was my teacher and she was very able. But when her pupils went to Tirane for the competition, we were always asked, "who was your teacher?" Then they said, "you are not able because your teacher cannot teach very well." And immediately they dismissed us. There is rivalry between the teachers of Tirane and the teacher in Shkoder. For about eight years no pupils of this school, in pianoforte, had won in Tirane. It was impossible to win in this competition because there were a lot of intermediate people who said, for example, please help so-and-so because he is a cousin or a friend of mine, or something like that. The competition was not as it should be.

And now what do you do?

Now I am a waiter in a cafe. I have no possibility to continue studying music. I don't have a piano in my house and here [at the school] it is impossible. Until this interview tonight, I have not played for one year.

Arben Zeneli at the Preng
Jakova Music School, Shkoder.

MY NAME IS PELLUMB GRISHAJ, I am twenty four; I was born in Lepushe on February 4, 1970. I went to the high school in Shkoder from 1984 to 1988. Then I studied at the Pedagogical Institute to become a teacher, and after that I started working as a as a teacher. And then, after a year, I started my studies by correspondence, working at the same time. Now I am in the last year of the university. I have three more exams left. I am studying Albanian language and literature. Because of the system of distributing books, it is very difficult to find books in this area. But I used to buy books in Shkoder, mainly when I was a student there. And I have continued to buy books thereafter, little by little. That's how I have come to have the library you see here. My special interest is in the field of literature, not only because I study it now, but because I have always loved it and I spend most of my free time with it. But I like music very much, too, especially symphonic music: Bach, Verdi, Mozart. I have a lot of friends here in Lepushe, but I can't talk about music or literature with them because they are not highly educated. This place is very far away from the city, and it is difficult to find people to discuss things I am interested in.

This is my sixth year of working as a teacher. Five years in Lepushe and this last year as the principal of the Vermoshi school. As director of the school in Vermoshe, I have a lot of responsibilities. Traveling to and from school has been one of my major difficulties, as there are no means of transportation. I usually walk. As for the school, I have a staff of fifteen people: twelve teachers, two kindergarten nurses and a school guard. Our main problem has always been the material base for teaching.

How do you help the teachers to adapt to the new curriculum, the change in the materials?

My help has consisted in giving them my pedagogical and professional experience and being close to them and discussing the teaching methods with them. This has been especially important for the teachers who do not have proper qualifications. They are given more advice on the pedagogical strategy than on the scientific concepts of the subjects they teach. There have been changes these two last years. A new way of constructing the class hour has been introduced. Until recently the teacher spoke and the students listened, while now there is a new method, that of the teacher leading the students to work by themselves. The students are objects and subjects at the same time. We have almost done away with the traditional methods of teaching and we are introducing new, European methods.

Do you like your work?

I used to like it at the beginning, but in these three last years, as things have changed, I don't like it as much. The teacher is not given his proper position in society. His salary is very low and the students are not interested in school. All this has made me lose some of my interest in and respect for the profession of the teacher. Our main problem is that a lot of the students don't attend school regularly or have abandoned it altogether, at a time when the law clearly states that education is compulsory. The teacher is confronted with the students' and their parents' indifference. Another problem is that of very slow students. The progress of the student during the school year depends very much on the teacher, because the student is generally considered to be a reflection of his teacher's work.

What would you like for your future?

I am not very ambitious for my future. In my early youth I dreamt of being an actor, while now I'd like to undertake modest steps in literature, going towards writing serious work. But literature is a difficult field and I can't foresee what will happen. It is not the same as in mathematics or business, where someone has to fulfill some premises and things get clear after that. In literature one has to encounter different difficulties and that's why it is more a wish than a hope. I don't want to treat any particular subject in my works. I prefer the meditative and philosophical side of literature.

Pellumb Grishaj with his library, Lepushe.

I'd like to write a work in which reality is presented allegorically. Franz Kafka is a perfect example of this kind of literature.

Could you say a few things about how you see Albania changing and some of the problems that are arising with these changes?

There are many great changes, especially in concepts and ideas which have been forged for fifty years. The people have to analyze the old concepts and change them. This is the main difficulty. For example, for fifty years the previous system dictated a certain way of living. People used to dress the same, think the same, while now, in the era of democracy, everyone is free to think in his own way, free to find the place he or she belongs to in the society. As another example, we are changing the idea that all the world is an enemy of our country and only we are going in the right direction. Another big problem is that of our nation. Our nation has a long and painful history. It is divided in two parts, one within the state boundaries and the other part in Yugoslavia. Generations of writers, for more than eighty years, have been working for the unification of our nation and I hope that now, in democracy, we can reunite the Albanian nation with the help of Europe and the United States.

Pellumb Grishaj outside the school in which he formerly taught, Budaç.

I AM GJOKE VERRISHTA, from Thethi; I am the principal of the school here. There are one hundred and seventy four children in the school, aged six to eighteen years. In the high school the students are taught mathematics, physics, biology, astronomy, and some other technical subjects on the construction of machines. Generally, people here are eager to learn. When they don't come to school, that is because there are no proper conditions here, no equipment, no books, no notebooks, no materials that can be used at school. Sometimes, with no school materials, they consider coming to school as time lost. But lately they are becoming more and more interested in school, because more books are available now. Still, there are a number of students who don't come. The main problem we have is the condition of the school. There is a stove for each classroom in the winter, but the classrooms cannot be heated because there is no glass in the windows, the doors are broken and it is difficult for the students to stay six hours a day at school in these conditions. The school building is badly damaged.

What do your students do after finishing this school?

Some of our students go to business school; some others to pedagogical school; some of them like to work on tourism, because our village has very good conditions for developing tourism. Tourists are attracted by the beautiful

Gjoke Verrishta, school principal, Theth.

landscape, by the fresh air and the very cold water that comes from the springs everywhere. And tourism is a very profitable business. We hope to have some powerful companies come here and construct new buildings. Lately some government-owned buildings were purchased by private individuals. They plan to employ people and develop tourism by making use of everything the village can provide for them.

We can have winter as well as summer tourism, because there are very good places for skiing and for camping and the tourists might like it. Now the road is closed in the winter because of avalanches in some places. But if there are investments in the future, the roads will be opened. And this would be better for tourism as well as for the village.

Flora Grishaj leads her flock of sheep down from the mountain, Lepushe.

MY NAME IS FLORA GRISHAJ; I was born in Lepushe in 1973. I started elementary school at the age of five. From then on I have continued studying with students older than myself, with good results so far.

When did you decide to become a veterinarian?

Since I was a child I wanted to become a doctor for humans, not a doctor for animals. I followed the high school veterinary studies, though this was not what I wanted to do. We were not given the chance to study what we wanted to, but what the government wanted us to study. And in the same way I had to go on and study at the university the same subject I had studied at high school. As I have been studying this subject for eight years, I have started to like it. And, as the physiology of animals is similar to that of human beings, I can surely say that I know something about humans, too.

I like both the city and the country. They both have their special things. I like the city for its culture, its development, and for the better conditions of life there. But I love the country, too, though it is somewhat difficult to live there. I like the country for the quiet life you can lead there, but as for the people, they are very backward. It is hard for me to find people here that have the same cultural background as me. This village is too far from the city and that is the reason that people here don't understand me. After all, a village is just a village. I can't say that I want to live in Tirane, but I can't say that I want to live in Lepushe, either. You know, I am at a stage of my life when it is difficult to decide where to live.

What will you do after you finish?

I'd like to open a private clinic. But I know that it is very difficult. I don't know yet the answer to your question. Let's take for example my classmates in Tirane. There are seventeen boys and three girls in my class. All the boys plan to work in a clinic or to emigrate abroad; most of them think about emigration as a possibility. As for the girls, they don't seem to have any clear perspective. All I can say is that I know my profession and I love it. And if I am going to have a chance to practice it with someone who has a large clinic of cows, sheep, and who is going to support me, it will not be difficult at all for me. While if I'm going to work here, where everyone has only one or two cows, and where I am supposed to travel from Lepusha to Tamare and Vermosh, that would really be very difficult.

What would you like – if you could choose certain things for yourself, for your future?

It is a private matter, but I can tell you something. Above all, I prefer a quiet life. That's why I wouldn't like a large family, with too many people in it. I'd like to work because I can't imagine myself without an occupation. I'd like to live in a civilized environment, because I can't imagine myself living all my life in a distant, forgotten place. So I would like to have a job, to have my own car and other things that I don't have now.

It's difficult to have a life that has the best of the city, the best of the country . . .

Let's hope.

MY NAME IS VIOLLCA OSJA, I study at the university, in the third year for Albanian language and literature. I like poetry and I write poetry. Now I am in school – today I will take the examination. Then I must decide how I will spend the holiday. I would like to continue studying Spanish because I want to take for my diploma the great writers of Colombia, such as Gabriel Garcia Marquez.

I like Albanian literature and the foreign literature. I like Russian literature, from Russia I like Pushkin – he's a great poet, Lermontov, and other poets. For example from Italy – Ungaretti, Quasimodo, in fact, these poets haven't been translated into Albanian and I am trying to translate some of them. From England I like Thomas Elliot, Walt Whitman, whose book you gave to me, and others. I like writers such as Virginia Wolff – I have read some by this author. James Joyce, in fact he's from Ireland, I know, but he is included in the British literature. And I like poets from America such as Ezra Pound – I read some poetry by this poet and I like it very much. Albania has great poets – I prefer Lazgush Poradeci, Migjeni. They are the great poets of Albania, but they lived in different times. Migjeni died very early; I think he was twenty seven years old. While Lazgushi died recently, in 1987.

Who are the great writers of Albania?

The greatest writer of Albania, in the opinion of all Albania, and of the world, is Ismail Kadare. In fact, I don't like Ismail Kadare so much. I like him, but not so much. But he is a great writer. Another great writer is Dritero Agolli. At this time we have many, many writers. I like a poet from Kosova – his name is Ali Podrimja – he is a great poet. But I think that Lazgush Poradeci and Migjeni are the greatest poets of Albania. Alesh Coleti is a great writer – I read some of his novels and I liked them very much. He is the publisher of *Playot,* one of the most interesting magazines abroad. The name means "generation." It is published in Italy. He published this magazine for approximately seventeen years. Another great poet, I forgot before, is Martin Camaj.

Is it possible now to buy the books and poems of these writers here in Shkoder?

I am trying to buy them, but sometimes I can't get them. Before, it was impossible to buy Martin Camaj's works because they couldn't be published in Albania. I have one of Martin Camaj's books – it's a gift of the author. The poetry is in the Albanian language and in German. He is not my favorite poet – but surely he is a great poet.

We hear that you won a prize from the Soros Foundation for your poetry.

I have won three prizes. One is a national prize from the youth organization, sponsored by the Soros Foundation. Then I won two prizes locally: when Shkodra organized a meeting for poetry, I won a second prize, and I won the first prize for poetry when the university organized another meeting for poetry. I would like to publish a book of my poetry in the future, but I haven't the money now.

*Opposite: Viollca Osja in her
room at home, Shkoder.*

An English Class (girls, ages twelve to sixteen, Shkoder)

O NE QUESTION *that is very important in America is the influence of television on young people. We talk about it a lot and are concerned about it, and we wonder what you think about it here.*

ENGLISH TEACHER: Think it over and give your own opinion about the influence of TV on young people, especially MTV.

FIRST STUDENT: I watch three or four hours on TV every day. But it isn't useful because what is on the TV isn't in our daily lives. I like only to hear the music.

ENGLISH TEACHER: Sorry to interrupt, but what about the content of the song? You like the music, the sound, but the content is another thing.

FIRST STUDENT: I look on TV, especially the titles, because they are in English and I can understand something.

ENGLISH TEACHER: So you are interested more in English than in the songs.

FIRST STUDENT: I like very much to hear the songs in English because they help me to learn much about the English language and they have more words that need us to speak more English language.

ENGLISH TEACHER: What do you think of Michael Jackson?

SECOND STUDENT: I like very much.

ENGLISH TEACHER: Listen to me! He is considered in America as a homosexual person, and MTV uses this actor as a mine of property, as a mine of wealth.

SECOND STUDENT: I like him as a singer, but not as a man.

ENGLISH TEACHER: Not as a man in the daily life. Thank you.

THIRD STUDENT: I watch everything that program, and I like it very much. I hear all songs and I understand some of them and I am very glad from that.

FOURTH STUDENT: I see TV all the days, only to practice, to practice the English language. I like all the American singers, but I have a special sympathy for Elvis Presley.

ENGLISH TEACHER: What about Madonna?

THIRD STUDENT: I like her songs but not like a person.

ENGLISH TEACHER: What about "Papa Don't Preach"?

THIRD STUDENT: I like that song very much.

FOURTH STUDENT: I like Elvis Presley and I don't believe that he has died.

*Along the road
from Bregu i
Lumit to Theth.*

A School Official in Shkoder

*W*E MET A YOUNG MAN *in the mountains who teaches English in Theth and lives in Bregu i Lumit. He has to walk three hours to work every day and three hours back. He would like to teach English in Bregu i Lumit instead, but there they teach only French. Would he have to get permission from Shkodra to teach English in his own village?*

We didn't have foreign language teaching in some villages until some years ago. In other villages students were taught Russian, while in the last years they have started teaching English, French, German or Italian. Now English is the main foreign language taught in every town school. As for the villages, some of their schools teach English and some others French. It depends upon the number of teachers available and ready to go and work in the villages. Our aim is to teach English almost in every school, but this is very difficult, because we have no possibilities to do that, we have no teachers.

But in this case, there is a teacher. The question is: "Who gives the permission to teach the subject? Can the director of the school in Bregu i Lumit decide or must Shkodra decide?"

In my opinion all the parents would like their kids to be taught English in all the schools. And the parents all over the country would prefer their children to start learning English in the first grade; this is true even for the most remote zones, where we cannot provide enough educated teachers even for other subjects. This year, the University of Shkoder is going to open a department for the English language, so we consider ourselves lucky that teachers of English will be prepared there. But it will take some time. It is a problem we cannot solve immediately. This year the first twenty five students will start their studies in the Department of English. After graduation they will be working for the schools of the city of Shkoder and other towns in the north.

Rrok Marku continues

NOW THAT I HAVE BECOME NINETY YEARS OLD, I have learned where America and where all the world is, through television. And some others have had the chance to visit the world, too. My daughter's son is now living in America. Two sons have gone to New York with their children and their wives. It is two or three years now that they have gone there. Also my daughter has gone there, with her husband, to stay for a couple of months. I have started to think of going out to see the world now, at this age. So, this is the world. Times change. If you are healthy, you manage everything. The good one is able to find his place.

Now we know that we are in good relations to the world, that we are having relations with other kingdoms. And those who have come from abroad have brought aid to us. We have to be thankful to them. What this country needs is workers. It needs people to work for it. It always had needed workers. We have been used to dealing only with animals. The shops and the new businesses have started only recently. They weren't before. Everything else there was, besides the animals, was in the hands of the government. We are a small country, but we have always been smart and good. But, as you see now . . . We are very glad to see you here with us. Please, drink some *raki*. To your health. May you have a good time here. May God help you. May you have honor and health, because that's the best thing of all.

Long life to your children!

*Rrok Marku and
his family, Grizhe.*

Postscript, 1997: Transition, or Tragedy?

WE RETURNED TO ALBANIA in August 1996, eager to see our many friends and to learn how they were faring. Tirane was noisier, more crowded, more chaotic, and more polluted than two years before. It was also a magnet, attracting not only the poor and the dispossessed but also intellectuals and young people from all over the country eager to be where the action was. Other cities we visited – Gjirokaster, Korçe, and Bajram Curri – seemed empty. But Shkoder had not changed very much. Its tradition of warmth and hospitality were still strong. There was now a beautiful but oversized white mosque in the center of town; it had been in the early stages of construction when we left. With the lifting of the embargo against ex-Yugoslavia, oil trucks no longer plied "the trade," but illegal commerce via Lake Shkoder continued, more quietly. The pace of downtown business had picked up, though in what seemed to us rather odd ways: for example, Shkoder somehow managed to support sixteen photo finishing studios. The parks were still grassy and still thronged in the evenings. They had not been paved over with kiosks and cafes, as had the parks in Tirane. There were many new restaurants, some air-conditioned, and the ice cream in the street stands had improved enormously.

Domestic life had become a little easier for many of our friends: Turkish bathrooms had been upgraded with modern fixtures, kitchens had been remodeled, old lumpy mattresses replaced with more comfortable ones. A few had traveled abroad, acquiring a wider lens through which to view their own society. But their new prosperity seemed to have been built on quicksand. Everything individuals could do to improve their own lives, they had done; anything the goverment might have done to support and sustain those lives, it had not done. In 1992 we were appalled that our friends in Tirane and Shkoder had running water only one or two hours a day (usually about 3 a.m.). This situation is temporary, they insisted: the old pipes cannot handle the increased demand, but they will soon be replaced, and we will have water twenty four hours a day. In 1994 there was still little or no water, but again we were assured that this would soon be fixed. By 1996, some people had managed to save enough money to buy water tanks that could be filled when (and if) the water ran, so that sometimes they indeed had water throughout the day. We were outraged; why weren't they? It was much the same story with electric power, roads, the telephone system, and other aspects of the infrastructure, which are necessary not only for individual comfort, but also for public health and for economic investment. Indeed, an economic base was almost wholly lacking, although (or because) Albania had been a model pupil of the International Monetary Fund. Retail trade of imported goods was booming, the cafes were always full, but almost nothing was being produced in Albania. Cash was flowing, but where was it really coming from? And where was it really going?

In fact, Albania in 1996 was a troubled society, despite its superficial progress. Many if not most of the people we spoke with, including prosperous ones, were frightened for the future. Political and economic problems loomed large, and were deeply intertwined. The May 1996 parliamentary elections, had been – to use polite language – "deeply flawed." Albania had somehow lost its way, not only on the road to democracy but on the road to a market economy as well. The rapid growth of pyramid schemes and rumors of their links to illegal trade and organized crime were alarming.

As we go to press, the schemes are collapsing and the country is in anguish; whether this is a twisted detour in Albania's transition to democracy or another episode in its continuing historical tragedy, is a story yet to be told. We hope this book will help you to understand the pain, and the dreams, that lie behind the headlines.

Glossary

A few words about Albanian

The Albanian language is a very ancient one; many scholars believe that it has evolved from Illyrian. It has no relatives (although it does belong to the Indo-European family of languages).

Albanian – called *shqip* in Albanian itself – is generally considered difficult for foreigners, especially English-speaking ones. Albanian grammar is highly complex. However, unlike English, the language is phonetic – once you learn to pronounce the sounds of the letters, you will rarely be in doubt as to how to pronounce the words in which they occur.

The alphabet is based on the Latin: a, b, c, ç, d, dh, e, ë, f, g, gj, h, i, j, k, l, ll, m, n, nj, o, p, q, r, rr, s, sh, t, th, u, v, x, xh, y, z, zh. Some of the sounds are similar to those of American English, but there are many important exceptions:

Albanian letter	American sound	as in . . .
a	ah	jar
c	ts	pits
ç	ch	champion
dh	th	this
ë	uh (or silent)	the
gj	gi	magician
i	ee	feet
j	y	yam
l	l	leaf
ll	l	cool
nj	ny	canyon
q	—	between sh and ch
r	—	the British 'very'
rr	—	trilled r
th	th	thank
u	oo	moon
x	x	first x in xerox
xh	g,j	gem, jam
y	ew	new
zh	su	pleasure

Several good Albanian language texts are available in the United States (see below). Here we will only mention the one feature of the language that you need to be aware of in order to understand the forms in which Albanian names appear in this book.

In Albanian, the ending of a noun depends on whether it is used in the definite or indefinite sense (and also on its role in the sentence). Thus "Tarabosh mountain is not high" would be "M*ali* i Taraboshit nuk është i lartë" while the more general "This mountain is not high" would be "Ky *mal* nuk është i lartë." The use of the definite and indefinite forms corresponds roughly (but not exactly) to the use of "the" and "a" in English.

However, not only nouns but also *proper names* have definite and indefinite forms; this is perhaps the most difficult feature of the language for native speakers of English to master, since the concept of indefinite proper names does not exist in English. (Albanians encounter the opposite problem in learning English.) Which form is used depends partly on whether the named person or place is the actor or plays a passive role; it also depends on the role of the name in the sentence. When, for example, Lucia Serreqi says "Moise's father *Zhak . . . Zhaku* moved to Shkoder . . . " she is using the indefinite form in the first instance and the definite form in the second. As another example, in Albanian one says that one is from *Tirana* or that one lives in *Tirane*. We have used only indefinite forms in the introductory essays (thus we say Shkoder, not Shkodra; Tirane, not Tirana, Durres, not Durresi), but in transcribing conversations we have given the forms actually used by the speaker. However, as is customary in transliteration, we have changed the *ë's* to *e's* throughout. In dictionaries Albanian nouns are listed in the singular indefinite.

A few words of Albanian

The following words appear in Albanian in the text.

bajrak	banner, or standard; a group consisting of several of *fises*
bajraktar	a leader of a *bajrak*
beg (bey)	an honorary title in the Ottoman Empire
besa	solemn oath, unbreakable pledge
besa e katundit	a solemn oath pledged by the members of a village
biografi	biography (used also in the sense of "personal history" or family background)
cifteli	a very long-necked two-stringed instrument, reminiscent of the dulcimer
ciftelik	large estates in the Ottoman Empire
fis	a group consisting of one or more extended families
kanun	a word of Turkish origin, meaning code of law, or canon
korit	a verb meaning "to be dishonored"
kuigji	the silversmith
lahute	a single-stringed musical instrument, used as accompaniment to epic songs and ballads
matrapas	a Turkish word meaning business speculator
medrese	Islamic religious school
parmende	wooden plow
pasha	an honorary title in the Ottoman Empire
raki	a strong brandy made (often at home) from plums, grapes, or mulberries
rapsod	a singer of epic songs and ballads
sandjak	an administrative unit in the Ottoman Empire

sherbel	a medicinal herb, a variety of sage (*Salvia officionalis L.*)
Sigurimi	security force (secret police)
shqip	the Albanian word for the Albanian language
shqiperia	the Albanian word for Albania
shqiptare	the Albanian word for Albanians
timar	land granted as a reward for service (in the Ottoman Empire)
vilayet	a smaller unit in a *sandjak*

Note: **dukla, gerokuli, shtara**, and **sanza** are local names for certain plants in Dukagjin. We do not know their English translations.

Latin and other italicized words that appear in the text

andart	a Greek word meaning guerilla fighter
Canis lupus	Gray wolf
Rupicapra rupicapra	chamois (a species of goat antelope)
Sciurus vulgaris	Red squirrel
Talpa europea	European mole

To learn Albanian (some introductory materials)

LUDMILA BUXHELI, *Speak and Read Essential Albanian*, Compact Edition, Pimsleur International, Inc., Concord, 1994. A programmed self-instructional course (ten lessons on five cassettes).

ISA ZYMBERI, *Colloquial Albanian*, Routledge Ltd., London and New York, 1991. A complete language text; a cassette is available separately. ISBN 0-415-05663-2

CEZAR KURTI, *Learn Albanian*, Legas Publishers, New York, 1995. ISBN 1-88190109-2

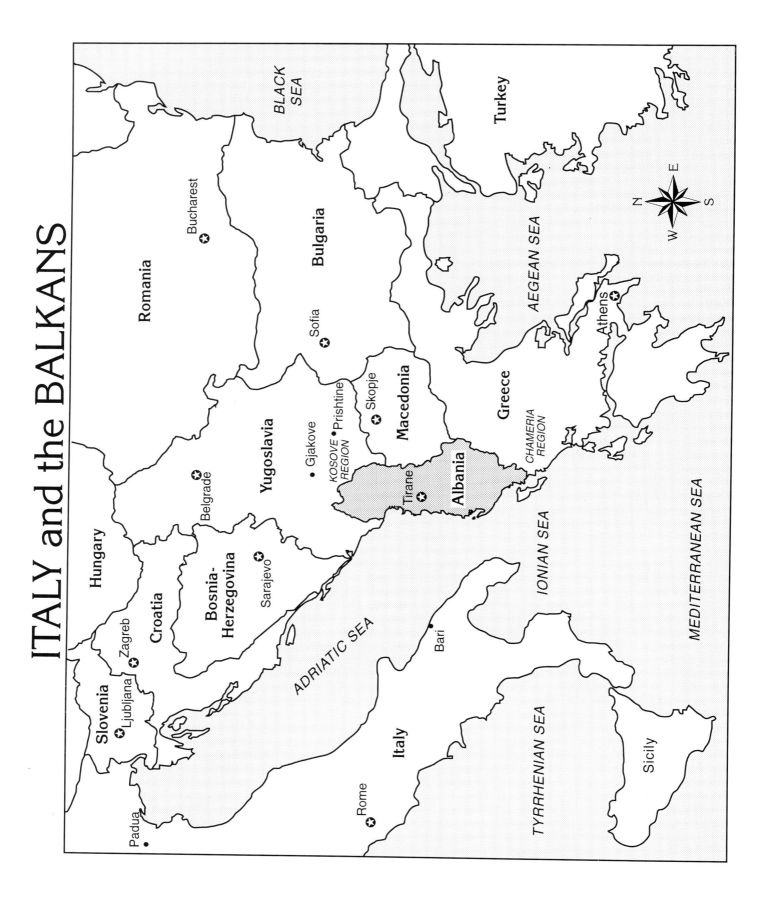

ITALY and the BALKANS

BLACK SEA

Turkey

Bucharest

Romania

Bulgaria

AEGEAN SEA

Sofia

Skopje

Macedonia

Athens

Yugoslavia

Gjakove

Prishtine

KOSOVE
REGION

Greece

CHAMERIA
REGION

Belgrade

Tirane

Albania

Hungary

Bosnia-
Herzegovina

Sarajevo

IONIAN SEA

MEDITERRANEAN SEA

Croatia

Zagreb

ADRIATIC SEA

Bari

Slovenia

Ljubljana

Italy

TYRRHENIAN SEA

Sicily

Padua

Rome

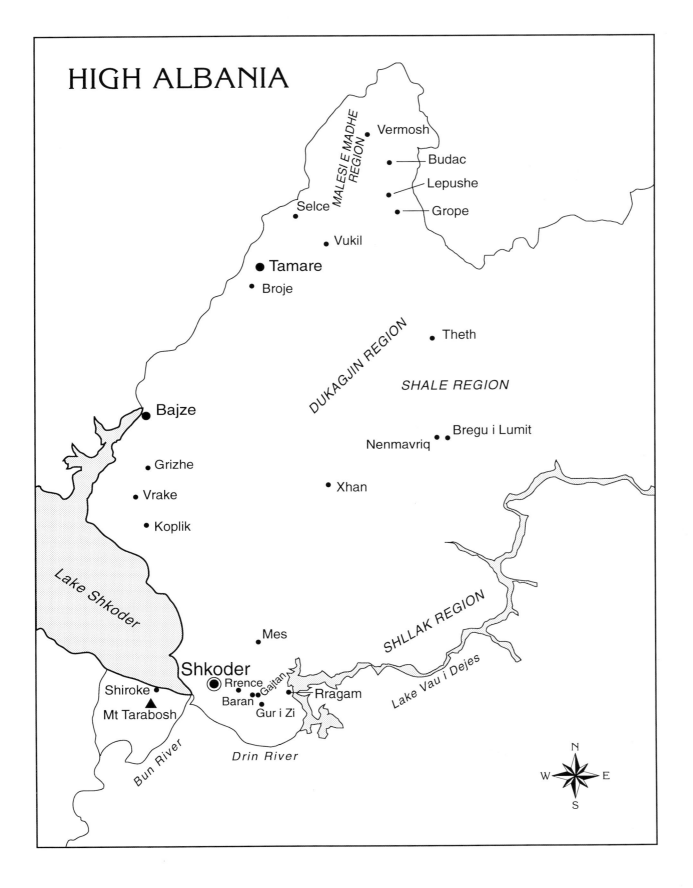

HIGH ALBANIA

MALESI E MADHE REGION

Vermosh

Budac

Lepushe

Selce

Grope

Vukil

Tamare

Broje

Theth

DUKAGJIN REGION

SHALE REGION

Bajze

Bregu i Lumit

Nenmavriq

Grizhe

Xhan

Vrake

Koplik

Lake Shkoder

SHLLAK REGION

Mes

Shkoder

Rrence

Gajtan

Shiroke

Rragam

Baran

Gur i Zi

Lake Vau i Dejes

Mt Tarabosh

Bun River

Drin River

N
W E
S

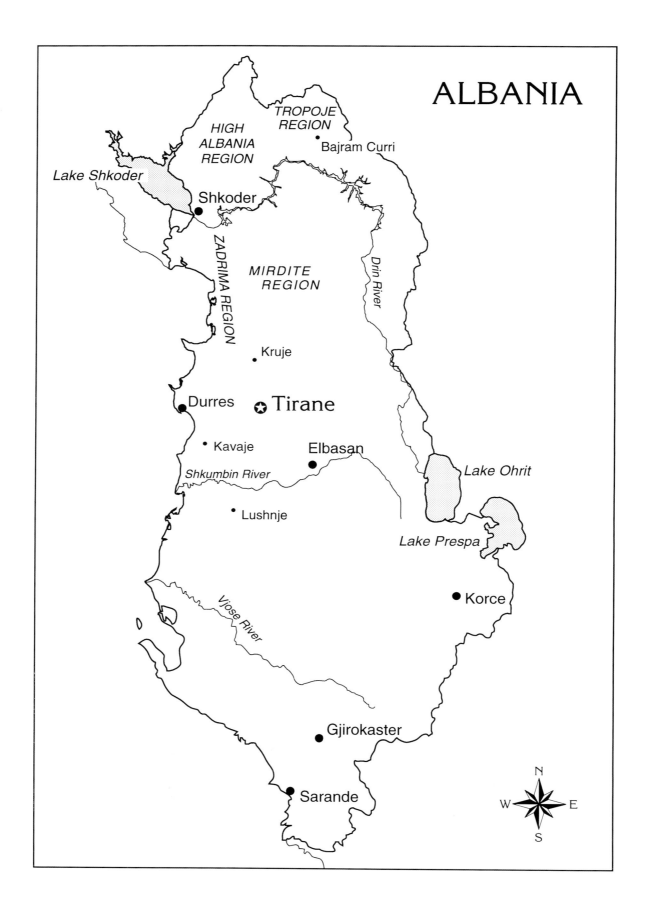

ALBANIA

TROPOJE REGION

HIGH ALBANIA REGION

Bajram Curri

Lake Shkoder

Shkoder

ZADRIMA REGION

MIRDITE REGION

Drin River

Kruje

Durres

Tirane

Kavaje

Elbasan

Lake Ohrit

Shkumbin River

Lushnje

Lake Prespa

Vjose River

Korce

Gjirokaster

Sarande

Bibliography

The list below contains an eclectic mix of books and articles that we have found helpful and/or interesting. To keep it to a reasonable size, only works in English (or in English translation) are cited here.

Travels and Travelers

ED2   JOHN B. ALLCOCK and ANTONIA YOUNG (eds), *Black Lambs and Grey Falcons: women travellers in the Balkans*, Bradford University Press, 1991

EDITH DURHAM, *High Albania*, London, Edward Arnold, 1909 (reprinted by Ayer Company Publishers Inc., 1994)

JAN and CORA GORDON, *Two Vagabonds in Albania*

ROSE WILDER LANE, *The Peaks of Shala*, New York and London, Harper & Brothers, 1923

JOSEPH SWIRE, *King Zog's Albania*, London, R. Hale and Company, 1937

Albania Today

JP   JAMES PETTIFER, *The Blue Guide: Albania*, London, A&C Black, 1994

FRANCES TRIX, "The Resurfacing of Islam in Albania," *East European Quarterly*, XXVIII, No. 4, 1995, pp. 533-549

HDR   HUMAN DEVELOPMENT REPORT, *Albania 1995*, United Nations Development Program, Tirana, 1995

History

NICOLAS BETHELL, *The Great Betrayal: the untold story of Kim Philby's biggest coup*, London, Hodder and Stoughton, 1984, reprinted by Times Books (New York), 1985

EDITH DURHAM, *The Struggle for Scutari*, London, Edward Arnold, 1914

GG   GIACOMO GARDIN, S.J., *Banishing God in Albania: the prison memoirs of Giacomo Gardin, S.J.*, San Francisco, Ignatius Press, 1988

JM   JAN MYRDAL AND GUN KESSLE, *Albania Defiant*, New York and London, The Monthly Review Press, 1976

DONALD M. NICOL, *Byzantium and Venice: a study in diplomatic and cultural relations*, Cambridge, Cambridge University Press, 1988

FAN S. NOLI, *George Castroiti Scanderbeg (1405-1468)*, New York, International Universities Press, 1947

NP   NICK PANO, "Albania," in *The Columbia History of Eastern Europe*, edited by Joseph Held

STEFANAQ POLLO and ARGEN PUTO, *The History of Albania from its Origins to the Present Day*, London, Routledge & Kegan Paul Ltd., 1981

HARVEY SARNER, *The Jews of Albania*, The Brunswick Press, distributed by the The Frosina Foundation, Boston, 1992

SS1 STAVRO SKENDI, *The Albanian National Awakening*, Princeton, Princeton University Press, 1967

MIRANDA VICKERS, *The Albanians: a modern history*, London and New York, I.B. Tauris, 1995

JW JOHN WILKES, *The Illyrians, Oxford*, UK & Cambridge USA, Blackwell, 1992

Cultural and Anthropological Studies

CARLETON COON, *The Mountains of Giants: a racial and cultural study of the North Albanian mountain Ghegs*, Papers of the Peabody Museum of American Archaeology and Ethnology, Harvard University, Volume. XXIII, No. 3 (Cambridge, Massachusetts, 1950)

EDI EDITH DURHAM, *Some Tribal Origins, Laws, and Customs of the Balkans*, London, George Allen & Unwin, Ltd., 1928

EDITH DURHAM, *The Burden of the Balkans,* London, Nelson, 1905

TS TROIAN STOIANOVICH, *Balkan Worlds: the first and last Europe*, Armonk, NY and London, England, M.E. Sharpe, 1994

ANTON FISTANI, *Human Evolution in Albania for the Quaternary Period*, pp. 141-178; in B*efore the Wall Fell, The Science of Man in Socialist Europe*, Edited by B.A. Sigmon, Toronto, 1993

Albanian Literature

Code of Lekë Dukagjini, collected by Shtjefen Gjecov, translated by Leonard Fox, New York, The Gjonlekaj Publishing Company, 1989

SS2 STAVRO SKENDI, *Albanian and South Slavic Oral Epic Poetry*, Memoirs of the American Folklore Society, Volume 44, Philadelphia, 1954

MARTIN CAMAJ, *Selected poetry*, translated by Leonard Fox, New York, New York University Press, 1990

ROBERT ELSIE, editor and translator, *An Elusive Eagle Soars* (an anthology of Albanian poetry), UNESCO, London and Boston, Forest Books, 1993

ISMAIL KADARE, *Broken April*, New York, New Amsterdam Books, 1990

ISMAIL KADARE, *Chronicle in Stone,* New York, New Amsterdam Books, 1987

ISMAIL KADARE, *Doruntine,* New York, New Amsterdam Books, 1988

ISMAIL KADARE, *General of the Dead Army,* New York, New Amsterdam Books, 1991

Of related interest . . .

ALICE MUNRO, "Albanian Virgin," *Open Secrets,* New York, A.A. Knopf , 1994. [A short story that draws heavily on the material of EDI.]

WADHAM PEACOCK, *Albania, The Foundling State of Europe*, New York, D. Appleton and Co., 1914

FRANCES TRIX, *Spiritual Discourse: learning with an Islamic master,* Philadelphia, University of Pennsylvania Press, 1993 [Conversations with Baba Rexheb (1903-1995), an Albanian leader of the Bektashi order.]

PHILIP WARD, *Albania: a travel guide,* Cambridge, The Oleander Press, 1983 [written during the communist era, when travel by Westerners was carefully controlled]

RW REBECCA WEST, *Black Lamb and Grey Falcon: a journey through Yugoslavia,* New York, Viking Books, 1941, reprinted by Penguin Books [The classic portrait of Albania's Slavic neighbors.]

NEXHMIE ZAIMI, *Daughter of the Eagle: the autobiography of an Albanian girl,* New York, Ives Washburn Inc., 1937 [The story of a girlhood in southern Albania before World War II.]

Acknowledgments

IT IS A GREAT PLEASURE to thank the many people who have participated in the creation of this book.

On our first visit to Albania, in 1992, we had the good fortune to be the guests of Emil and Valentina Plumbi in Tirane, Zina Franja in Shkoder, and the Idrizi family in Gjirokaster. The warmth of their hospitality and the long, thoughtful, and stimulating conversations around their dining tables shaped our early image of and affection for Albania.

In 1994, we lived for three months with the extended Luli family in Shkoder. All of the Lulis – Matilde Luli, her sons, their wives, and her grandchildren (Gjovalin, Rosina, and their children Pjerin and Dori; Bernard, Antoneta, and their children Noel and Matilde; Angelin and Diana and their children Andreas and Ruben) welcomed us into their lives as well as their home, and helped us in every imaginable way.

We were also houseguests of Arben and Mimoza Kallamata in Tirane, Zef and Katerina Grishaj in Lepushe, Gjon and Eneda Bushaj in Selce, Pellumb and Ana Pepaj in Selce, Luk and Zoja Drini in Shale, and Gjoke, Ndue, and Tom Shyti in Theth; we are grateful to all of them for their warm and extended hospitality. Thanks are also due to Gjovalin Kolombi, Rector of University Luigj Gurakuqi in Shkoder, for facilitating our second visit to Albania.

All of our hosts and also our good friends Anton Fistani, Father Tedi Hochstatter, Gjergj Marena, Marije Sheldija, and Alma Tamarinda discussed many complex issues with us and helped to broaden our understanding of the things we saw and heard.

We met most of the people interviewed in this book through our Albanian friends, who went out of their way to introduce us to people whom they thought we would like and would find interesting. Zef Bushati, Anton Fistani, Prek Gilaj, Antoneta Luli, Dori Luli (then aged nine), Gjergj Marena, Marije Sheldija, and Rrok and Ardiana Smajlaj accompanied us to places near and far, and translated for us as well. After our return to the United States, Mimoza Kallamata listened to all of the tapes and provided us with verbatim English transcriptions. We are grateful to Mayor Filip Guraziu of Shkoder for permission to reproduce photographs from his rich historical collection.

Many friends and colleagues have read various drafts of the manuscript and have made invaluable suggestions, reflecting their varied professional expertise. It is a pleasure to thank Frank Columbus, Geti Fistani, Daniel Fitzgibbons, Patrick Gregory, Joel Halpern, Nelly Hoyt, Estelle Jussim, Arben and Mimoza Kallamata, Sokol and Ela Kondi, Marian Moody, John Nelson, Elliot Offner, Naum Prifti, Frances Trix, Luan Troxel, and Norma Wikler for their assistance. Kathleen Imholz has been a wonderful sounding board (and wonderful friend) throughout.

We are especially grateful to Anton Fistani and Barbara Kerewsky Halpern, who served as unofficial editors, correcting a myriad of details large and small.

Jim Burke, Karen Chrisman, Wayne Cournoyer, John Nelson, Elliot Offner, and Bruce Wilcox graciously shared their expertise with a novice book designer. Jack Harrison gently guided us through the many stages of designing this book, and beyond.

Elpinike Frasher has supported and encouraged us from the beginning of our interest in her native land to the present. It is difficult to express how much this has meant to us.

This project was made possible through a fellowship from the Council for International Exchange of Scholars (Fulbright). We are also grateful to Jeannette Mittelsdorf for her assistance.

Above all, we thank the many people in High Albania who so generously agreed to be photographed and allowed us record our conversations with them. No one requested anonymity: the decision to present some conversations anonymously was our own. For reasons of space, not everyone we spoke with could appear in this book, but their contributions are reflected in our appreciation of the Albanian people and their fascinating land.

230